THE
MAKING OF AMERICA
SERIES

COLUMBIA RIVER GORGE
NATURAL TREASURE ON THE OLD OREGON TRAIL

Enjoy!
Cheri Dohnal

One of the Gorge's fabulous falls, White River Falls is far off the beaten path. It is worth the extra trip to one of southern Wasco County's most awe-inspiring secrets. Photo by Charity Husk.

THE
MAKING OF AMERICA
SERIES

COLUMBIA RIVER GORGE

NATURAL TREASURE ON THE OLD OREGON TRAIL

CHERI DOHNAL

ARCADIA

Published by Arcadia Publishing
an imprint of Tempus Publishing Inc.
Charleston SC, Chicago, Portsmouth NH, San Francisco

Printed in Great Britain

Library of Congress Catalog Card Number: 2003109383

For all general information contact Arcadia Publishing at:
Telephone 843-853-2070
Fax 843-853-0044
E-Mail sales@arcadiapublishing.com
For customer service and orders:
Toll-Free 1-888-313-2665

Visit us on the Internet at http://www.arcadiapublishing.com

Front cover: *Lumberjack operations of the 1890s included several sturdy men, a few horses, several oxen, a couple of wagons, and several two-man hand saws up on a hillside. When the wagons were full, the felled trees were taken to a mill and unloaded.*

CONTENTS

Acknowledgments   6
Introduction   8

1.   Volcanoes and Other Violent Eruptions   11
2.   Part of the Trail, but no Settlers Allowed   18
3.   Wagons Ho! In their own Words   29
4.   More Indian Wars and a Super-sized County   46
5.   The Development Years   59
6.   Carving a Niche in World Economics   70
7.   Tragedy and Triumph: Testing the Pioneer Spirit   81
8.   Pack Trains and Stagecoaches   95
9.   War, Prohibition, Automation, and Modernization   106
10. Making Connections and Entertaining Dignitaries   121
11. Columbia Rolls On Until Miss Helen Blows Her Top   132
12. Modern Pioneers Meet Guarded Guru   147

Appendix: Notable Gorgers   153
Bibliography   156
Index   159

ACKNOWLEDGMENTS

It is rare when the author of any historical volume is able to single-handedly gather all information and photos needed to produce an accurate yet entertaining work. This book is no exception to that rule. Many hours were contributed toward this volume by a long list of people who gathered photos, checked facts, dug through personal collections to provide pieces of the puzzle, and generally told the story of the Gorge's people. I am deeply indebted to those people, for without their support, this book might never have been published.

Some of the photos and stories herein were archived at various locations throughout the Pacific Northwest. A surprising number of contributions came directly from personal photo collections and family histories of individuals with ties to the Gorge. Without the assistance and cheerful cooperation of the following people and organizations, those resources would not have been accessible to me and therefore, to my readers.

Many thanks to the following individuals and the staffs of these businesses and organizations, for their cooperation and contributions: Rodger Nichols and Dan Spatz at *The Dalles Chronicle*, of whom I asked far too much; Barbara Cole and The Dalles Family History Center; Walt Davies; Cecil Houk; Barbara and Lisa Fenkner; Rahlie Goodall; Judy Savage Gyllenskog; Charity Husk; Jim Jerman; Ralph Keeney; Judy Livings; Connie Nice and the Hood River County Historical Museum; Toni McLaughlin; David and Ellen McNett; the Oregon Historical Society; the Oregon Historical Photo Collection (Salem Public library); the Oregon Trail Interpretive Center and Discovery Museum; Marlene Pointer; Lois Powell; Julie Schall; Helen Schunke; Southern Wasco County Library (SWCL) and SWCL Friends' League; Spokane (WA) Public Library; David E. Wieprecht at United States Geological Survey; Warm Springs Confederated Tribes; Wasco County Historical Society; and Dee Hill and Nancy Zopf at the Wasco County Pioneers' Association. Additional thanks goes to the United States Forest Service and the Oregon Department of Transportation, and very special thanks to the many old-timers of the Gorge who allowed me to ask them innumerable questions about their youthful years.

On a more personal level, Violet Moore Guy and Earline Wasser have both straddled the fence between supportive friend and helpful assistant throughout the years of hunting, gathering, fact-checking, and writing.

My parents Elvin and Marjorie (Al and Marge) Dohnal, brothers Rick and Todd Dohnal, and my children Jessi and Logan Winger all maintained a belief that I could take this project all the way to the finish line, and their encouragement has come in many different forms. If they could have, I'm sure that my new grandsons Gabriel Benjamin and Aidan Jacob would have given me the thumbs-up, too. Friends Sonia Norton Hintze, Scott McKim, and Michael E. Smith have all invested in this and my other manuscripts by providing support during one crisis or another. My former newspaper publisher Herb Swett was the impetus of my freelance career, for it was he who pointed me toward a way to keep writing when I was a busy young mother. A huge "thank you" goes to each of them.

Finally, I want to thank my editor Rob Kangas and publisher Christine Riley at Arcadia Publishing, who shared my enthusiasm about this project and kept things moving forward despite my computer failures and other obstacles. At Arcadia I've found a very professional, yet surprisingly friendly staff. I look forward to working with them again on future volumes about the Pacific Northwest.

It takes many people to bring any book to fruition. I am merely the messenger.

This little guy is unidentified, thus Dapper Dan is appropriate. The only thing known is that he lived in the Gorge around the turn of the century and was related to the Hurst family. Note the furry animal on wheels. Courtesy of Hurst family photo archives.

INTRODUCTION

Since the time of its discovery by Captain Robert Gray in 1792, the Columbia River has been a point of fascination for most who have had occasion to experience her. Named by Captain Gray for his ship, *Columbia Rediviva*, the river is a formidable opponent for those who challenge her even now. Dams and locks have tamed the river somewhat, but the intrigue of the Gorge remains.

To discuss the history of the Columbia River Gorge only since the arrival of the white man would be like building a mansion without benefit of a foundation. The Gorge's ancient past has everything to do with its present and the future of its people.

Covering an expanse 80 miles long and up to 4,000 feet deep, the canyon walls mark the boundary between the states of Oregon and Washington. The Gorge is home to more than 75,000 people and serves as a major transportation corridor to and from the Pacific Ocean. It is the only sea-level route through the Cascade Mountains. The river continues east and then north a total of 1,270 miles to its beginnings at Lake Columbia in British Columbia, Canada. Its major tributaries include the Kootenai, Flathead/Pend Oreille/Clark's Fork, Snake, and Willamette Rivers. Of those, the Snake River flows 1,038 miles from its origins in Yellowstone National Park in Wyoming, with the combination covering 2,308 miles.

The Gorge's features were formed as a result of a series of geologic events spanning millions of years. Although the area's physical features continue to be altered by geological factors outside the control of humankind, the focus of this book is the social evolution of the past 150-plus years. The Gorge's beauty is breathtaking and its natural resources plentiful. These assets did not escape the notice of even the earliest European explorers, and they were utilized extensively by Native Americans.

Lewis and Clark, during their first foray into the Pacific Northwest some 200 years ago, were impressed by what they saw but also limited by the same natural beauty. It was a difficult area for them to explore due to the unusually rugged terrain. This book seeks to expand on their limited Gorge explorations and continue the story up through the present.

In reading this book, some basic premises should be understood. The first centers around the fact that the Columbia River Gorge's social history begins a considerable period of time before the area was settled by white men. This part of Gorge history was documented only in oral stories and remains largely beyond our grasp to this day.

Several Native American tribes inhabited both sides of the Columbia River when white settlers began to pour into the area. As a result, a large proportion of the earliest caucasian pioneers had no choice but to settle first in the Willamette Valley on the west side of the Cascade mountain range when they came west. Nearly all of them passed through the Gorge on their way to western Oregon, but almost none came directly to begin their western lives in the Gorge during the 15 to 20 years of mass migration to Oregon country in the 1840s and 1850s. Those complications are explained in the first few chapters, where actual pioneer diaries and memoirs are used to allow the reader to enjoy a full knowledge of the journey itself, as well as early pioneer life and some of the challenges presented to the native tribes. Thus, some of the state's early history, as well as the pioneer journeys themselves, meld into the Gorge's history quite naturally.

The reader should also be aware that early Gorge history was recorded by very few truly objective parties. Relatively little about the earliest pioneer days of the Gorge was written in newspapers until the 1860s, since the nearest newspaper office was located on the west side of the Cascades. Even where it was recorded in the media of the day, the journalist was often presenting a biased point of view.

Although many basic facts were written exactly the same way by more than one person, much of the early history is subjective, and many conflicting "facts" were

Pine Grove school bus en route to the day's events, 1917. Jack Bayley, bus driver, students not identified. This was the good-weather configuration of the bus, which used a removable canopy shell during inclement weather. Note that this early Oldsmobile used a wagon box as its seating area. Photo courtesy of Hood River County Historical Museum.

recorded. Where the author has been able to find a reliable source telling a different story than the first, it has been included here. This doesn't mean study of the Gorge's social history has been an exact science, but hopefully this book will be a springboard that leads us all to a better understanding of how events unfolded.

Care has been taken to present an unbiased view of early conflicts between white settlers and the Native Americans who first inhabited the Gorge. Quotations, of course, reflect the actual viewpoint and wording of the person being quoted, which may contain politically incorrect or even offensive terminology. The reader will find expressions like "redskins" and "savages" within quotations on these pages. On the other hand, some facts given herein put the pioneers in a negative light. This is unavoidable if a factual history is to be told.

The reader may notice that the majority of the information in this book pertains more to the Oregon communities than places found in Washington. There are two reasons for this. First and foremost, there is a larger population along the Oregon shores of the Gorge and it was the side settled earlier by pioneers. The other reason is simply a limitation of space within my publisher's parameters. There is far too much history in the Gorge to fit it all into a single volume, and much of the Washington information had to be saved for the next book. It was the only logical way to portion things out for these purposes.

It is my hope that this book will be a way for both the pioneers and Native Americans to tell their own stories of those early years, filling in the gaps left by sketchy recording of the facts. The author should merely be history's narrator, rather than attempting to be its creator.

Katherine and Louise Frank take a buggy ride. Photo probably taken shortly before their father Charles's death in 1905. Courtesy of Barbara Fenkner.

1. VOLCANOES AND OTHER VIOLENT ERUPTIONS

The Gorge's story begins long before the arrival of the most ancient peoples. According to geologists who have studied its history, the Columbia River once took a different path. It occurred more than 17 million years ago, when the Gorge itself was nothing more than a flat stretch of land, a small portion of the Columbia River Plateau.

Between 6 and 17 million years ago, volcanic activity beneath the earth's surface created fissures that spewed molten basaltic lava, eventually covering a total of about 25,000 cubic miles of land in what is now Washington, Oregon, and western Idaho . Because this type of lava flow is extremely heavy, domes were not formed; instead, the magma cooled slowly in layers. The basalt is estimated to be as much as 3 miles thick in some places.

Later, the Cascade mountain range added another dimension to the Gorge. This range is composed of more than two dozen mountains and volcanoes stretching 700 miles north and south from Canada to the northern tip of California. The volcanic activity responsible for creating the Cascades also yielded a series of lava flows that further layered the landscape in sheets of basalt.

Average height of peaks in the Cascade Range is 5,000 feet above sea level. One of the most visible mountains is the 11,239-foot Mount Hood, its glacier-capped peak majestically jutting from the clouds above the Gorge's southern edge. Mount St. Helens, a Cascade Range volcano whose name and recent history will be familiar to most readers, is located a short distance north of the Columbia River from The Gorge. The geologic plates resulting in the formation of the Cascades are part of the Pacific "Ring of Fire."

If volcanic activity holds no interest for the reader, perhaps glacial flows will do the job, as the Gorge owes its history to those as well. The Columbia River Basin was formed 12,000 to 19,000 years ago, near the end of the last Ice Age. According to the USDA:

> Immense ice dams half a mile high held back melting ice, creating a huge lake in northwest Montana, called Lake Missoula. Each time the ice gave way (at least 40 times), massive walls of water as

high as 400 feet rushed seaward with great destructive force. These floods generally followed the route of the present day Columbia River.

The first documented history of the Gorge's people, however, begins with the indigenous communities of the Pacific Northwest about 11,000 years ago. Archaeological studies have found evidence of a civilization that took advantage of the great fishing and bountiful wild berries the area provided, even back then.

Near the location of what is now known as "Cascade Locks," there exists a geological oddity. Some 500 years ago, Native Americans who lived along the banks of the Columbia River witnessed an event of legendary proportions. In fact, those who lived to tell about it did pass down a fable to explain the freak occurrence.

A view of Mount Hood from one of the local orchards. Ben Gifford, photographer. Courtesy of Hood River County Historical Museum.

This legend has its factual beginnings during the above-mentioned floods, when a mountain on the Oregon side of the river apparently fell away into the riverbed. The landslide blocked the river's flow, linking what are now Oregon and Washington with a natural dam. Water backed up behind the dam, flooding the inland prairies as far away as western Idaho. Native tribes of the area called the dam "The Great Crossover," and it later became known as the "Bridge of the Gods."

There is evidence of a natural bridge, or at least part of one, that did exist at this location. Proof also exists that shows a part of the land now on the Washington side of the river was once part of the Oregon side, and vice versa. Furthermore, local Indians of the nineteenth century claimed to have ancestors who used the bridge to meet with others in a great tribal council, and it is a part of their oral history.

The geological formation leaves today's experts with many unanswered questions. Both science and legend would have us believe that the rock formations came together to form a bridge over the river—not simply a place where the river was rerouted, but an actual bridge where water ran under. Modern thought leads us to imagine an elevated arch above the water, but of course this is not what the natives saw.

Geological studies have shown that it probably began as a fairly solid land mass, more of a dam than a bridge, with enough seepage to allow water to exist on both sides of the bridge. Water pressure eventually eroded the rock and gravel dam, bursting through it with a generated force of up to 50-foot waves as the water rushed toward the sea. Many Native Americans undoubtedly lost their lives and there is some speculation that entire tribes may have been wiped out in the resulting flood, which also covered what is now Portland.

Only several large boulders remained of the dam, which created the Cascade Rapids, and a mound of smaller debris on the river's north side. A man-made bridge was constructed much later (1926) at the same location, its northern pilings anchored in the remnants of the natural bridge, aptly named "Bridge of the Gods." The Cascade Rapids were the impetus for naming the Cascade mountain range, although the rapids were eventually submerged in waters now held back by Bonneville Dam.

All legends about the Bridge of the Gods seem to hold a common thread, but specific details vary from one tribe to another. The common thread is found in the Great Spirit, who built the land bridge to allow native brothers to visit with one another. One of them fell in love with a beautiful maiden and all went well until the fair woman began to flirt with the other brother. Soon the siblings were fighting over the maiden's affections and the Great Spirit responded with a huge show of temper that destroyed the bridge.

One legend describes the story of two brothers, Klickitat and Wy'East, who competed for the affections of a beautiful maiden. The Great Spirit, Manito,

13

turned both brothers into mountains (Klickitat as Mount Adams in the north, and Wy'East as Mount Hood in the south) and put a homely woman named Loo-Wit in between to guard the bridge. The men insisted upon acting like fools, fighting over the beautiful maiden, flinging rocks and spewing hot coals in anger. Manito destroyed the bridge with a great shake of the earth, spewing boulders onto the bridge until it collapsed. Loo-Wit was so distressed about the situation, she asked Manito to make her youthful and beautiful again, and thus Manito turned her into Mount St. Helens.

Another version of the legend is that Manito, the Great Spirit, placed Loo-Wit, the wise old woman, on the bridge as its guardian and sent his sons to earth as great snow mountains. Multnomah was the warrior, Klickitat (Mount Adams) the totem pole maker, and Wy'East (Mount Hood) the singer. Peace and happiness prevailed until beautiful Squaw Mountain moved into a small valley between Klickitat and Wy'East. Thanks to the Evil One and some bad judgement (flirting) on the part of Squaw Mountain, the brothers were soon fighting. Although Squaw Mountain had grown to love Wy'East, she enjoyed flirting with Klickitat.

The brothers caused quite a commotion, growling and rumbling at one another. It escalated into stomping their feet and spewing fire and ash into the air, belching forth clouds of smoke so dark that the sun was not visible. They hurled rocks and spewed many flames, causing the forests to catch fire. After carrying on like this for some time, their stomping, shaking, and stone throwing caused the Bridge of the Gods to collapse and fall into the river. This so angered the Great Spirit that he shook the very foundation of earth, moving Squaw Mountain to a new location beside Klickitat. Squaw Mountain's heart was broken, for she truly loved Wy'East, so she fell at Klickitat's feet and sank into a deep slumber from which she could not be awakened. She is now called Sleeping Beauty and lies west of Mount Adams. Loo-Wit, guardian of the bridge, had executed her duties faithfully and as a reward Manito arranged for her to fall gently into the river with the bridge, later emerging as the young and beautiful Mount St. Helens.

No matter how ancient the civilization, it seems men have always been dueling over women and neither sex has lacked the ability to be flirtatious. One would have to wonder: if Loo-Wit became Mount St. Helens, what raised her ire to the point of eruption in 1980? Were those boys up to no good again?

Native tribes utilized the bountiful natural resources of the Gorge for centuries before the white man arrived. The most important of those resources were the Pacific Salmon, which make their way up the Columbia (N'ch-iwana) every year to spawn. The Gorge had the best fishing holes for many miles, so several different tribes made their homes along or near the river. Many other northwest tribes came long distances to join the local tribes near Celilo Falls for fishing and trading each year. Tribes that fished and traded along the Columbia included the Clallam, Klickitat, Cowlitz, Tillamook, Celilo (Wyam), Wishram,

An overview of the Native American fishing grounds surrounding Celilo Falls from the Oregon side. Note the platform construction. Courtesy of The Dalles Chronicle.

Wasco, Nisqually, Rogue, Umpqua, Chehalis, Calapooia, Shasta, Walla Walla, Chinook, Cayuse, Nez Perce and Snohomish Indians.

The Falls were full of salmon, but the combination of a fast current, a wide river, and the lack of accessible riverbanks posed a special problem. Never discouraged by natural obstacles, local tribesmen used some very creative postures for fishing in the less accessible areas nearest the Falls, hanging precariously over the edges of handmade platforms using long-handled, hand-woven dip nets to capture the salmon. In less hazardous locations they used nets and spears to fish from canoes and river banks. The Nez Perce used a different technique. They would launch a raft after dark, attract the fish to the surface with a lit torch to fool them into thinking the sun was rising, then spear dozens of fish by the time the raft reached its stopping point down river. They would be dragged back upstream repeatedly to start the next fishing run, several times throughout the night.

Native tribes were very well fed and clothed by using a wide variety of skills to capture and utilize an abundance of wild game, fish, roots, and berries offered by the Gorge's interesting combination of environments. They were able to travel relatively short distances up and down the river as the year progressed, moving their camps downstream to take advantage of wild berries growing in the more temperate but rainy sections, then upstream to partake of the prolific salmon supply each summer. Even when they chose to live in the more moderate climate of the western Gorge in winter, tribesmen were still close enough to hunt effectively for game that would normally be found in the more frigid mountain country.

It is little wonder then, that they became alarmed at the rapid influx of white pioneers in the 1840s and 1850s. As you will see in the following chapters, the native population and the intruding pioneers actually got along quite well with one another most of the time. Each had a healthy fear of the other while also having, as a whole, a reasonable respect for the heartbreak that might follow if one were to anger the other. In many cases, there was a genuine personal respect between a white man and his native brother.

Regardless of how they felt about each other, pioneers and native tribes had to learn to communicate in a common language. As a result, something known as the Chinook Trade Jargon came into use throughout the Pacific Northwest. It is a strange combination of English, French, and the languages of several native tribes, including Chinook, Nootka, and Salish, with a sprinkling of Wasco, Celilo, or Klickitat twists used only in the Columbia Gorge. Other locations in the Northwest had their own local variants, but the base language was widely used.

This dialect was so extensively used that in 1909 a dictionary was compiled by George C. Shaw and published in Seattle by the Rainier Printing Company. It is a fascinating language to explore, particularly for anyone who has lived in the Northwest for a number of years, because one can discover so many roots of our modern-day regional expressions in it. Here are but a few examples of this peculiar language. Some may be recognized by the reader in quotations used throughout the book, and others may be familiar to people whose family has lived anywhere in the Pacific Northwest. Chinook trade jargon in its written form is pronounced phonetically. How many do you recognize?

> Saghalie Tyee—the Great One, the Almighty
> heehee—amusement
> siam itchwoot—bear (grizzly)
> stickskin—bark (tree)
> siskiyou—bob-tailed (a bob-tailed horse)
> tumtum—to think, decide, or feel something, as in *mamook kloshe tumtum* (to make friends or peace), and *sick tumtum* (grief, jealousy)
> tyee—great one, superior, boss, king
> wawa—to speak, talk, or answer (*wawa kloshe wawa* means to eulogize)
> mahsh stone—to castrate
> memaloost or mimoluse—dead
> bebe—kiss

siwash—Indian

kloshe tumtum or kahkwa tillikum—friendly

muck-a-muck—to eat or take something into the mouth

mitlite tenas kopa yaka belly—pregnant

saghalie—up high or in the sky

Both a petroglyph (a design carved into rock) and pictograph (drawn or painted onto rock), Tsagaglalal, or "She Who Watches," sits atop a large rock mound at Horsethief State Park, overseeing all activity on the river.

2. Part of the Trail, but No Settlers Allowed

Only a handful of purposeful souls came to the Oregon Territory as explorers or to establish trading posts and missions between 1805 and 1841. The vast majority were members of the Hudson's Bay party, and few stayed beyond the lucrative trading post days of the 1840s. Missionaries were in place to minister to the perceived spiritual needs of the native population, but most had no plans to guide the impending influx of immigrants.

When Lewis and Clark made their way westward, they traveled through Idaho and Washington and arrived at the mouth of the Columbia River in late October 1805. They made one encampment at the approximate point now known as Horsethief Lake State Park on the Washington side of the river, where the Wishram Indians made their home. This park is known by many as the one where visitors can see one of the most famous petroglyphs in the Pacific Northwest: "Tsagaglalal" or "She Who Watches." Because of the many rock formations there, they called the area Rock Fort in their journals.

The eruption of Mt. Hood earlier that year had filled the Columbia River and its tributaries with gritty volcanic ash, inspiring Clark to refer to the murky-looking Sandy River as "Quicksand River" in his journal. After making portage to save themselves from Celilo Falls, Captain Clark had the following to say about the next phase of their journey down the Columbia:

> In those narrows the water was agitated in a most Shocking manner boils Swell & whorl pools, we passed with great risque It being impossible to make a portage of the Canoes, about 2 miles lower passed a verry bad place between 2 rocks one large & in the middle of the river here our Canoes took in some water, I put all the men who Could not Swim on Shore; & sent a fiew articles Such as guns & papers, and landed at a village of 20 houses on the Stard. Side in a Deep bason where the river apprd. to be blocked up with emence rocks . . .

A few others ventured to the Oregon coast but none probably came through the Gorge until David Douglas and John Scouler came to peruse the plant life and take samples of it. Arriving by ship near the mouth of the Columbia, they set out to classify the botanical treasures of the Pacific Northwest and found many new species. In 1825 they toured the Gorge with their Indian guides on assignment for the Royal Horticultural Society of England. Mr. Douglas wrote of their adventures in his journal:

> As there was a strong easterly wind against us, we only gained 35 miles; camped 7 miles below the Grand Rapids; continued rain throughout. The following day made a portage over the Rapids and camped on a small stony island ten miles above them. Showery. At this season, the Rapids are seen to advantage, the river being low. The scenery at this season is likewise grand beyond description; the high mountains in the neighbourhood, which are for the most part covered with pines of several species, some of which grow to an enormous size, are all loaded with snow; the rainbow from the vapour of the agitated water, which rushes with furious rapidity over shattered rocks and through deep caverns producing an agreeable although at the same time a somewhat melancholy echo through the thick wooded valley; the reflections from the snow on the mountains, together with the vivid green of the gigantic pines, form a contract of rural grandeur that can scarcely be surpassed.

Douglas returned to England with some hard-won samples of plant life from the Cascades, but returned in 1830 with his Scottish Terrier, Billy. This visit was shorter and he continued his explorations down into California. Upon seeing the redwood trees, he wrote that something "plainly tells me we are not in Europe."

Majestic Mount Hood. Courtesy of Hood River County Historical Museum.

From there he took a ship to the Sandwich Islands (now called Hawaii) and returned to the Columbia on October 24, 1832. He wrote about the Columbia River, "This mighty stream is incomparably the noblest in the world for salmon, trout and sturgeon, whether for quality or abundance."

He passed through again in October of the same year and returned once more in July of 1833 to make the first known attempt to climb Mount Hood, returning once again to the Sandwich Islands to await his next trip to the Columbia. Almost precisely a year later he died from an apparent accidental fall into a pit used to trap wild bulls in the Sandwich Islands. Billy avoided the same fate somehow and lived the rest of his days on the British Isles.

Despite many setbacks, including repeated losses of collected specimens and seeds, Douglas managed to catalog and ship more than 200 new plant species to the British Isles during his odyssey in the New World. Thanks to his dedication, a large number of them are now permanent residents of England. Among the species he formally classified was a tree now known as Oregon's state tree, the Douglas Fir. Interestingly, it is not a fir at all nor was it classified as such by Douglas. Known in some parts of the world as the Oregon Pine, the Douglas Fir is known to botanists as a pseudotsuga, or false hemlock—a species in its own right. It grows to a height of 180 to 200 feet and a diameter of 4 to 6 feet, although trees as large as 325 feet tall and 10 to 15 feet in diameter have been found. Douglas also collected the seeds of Oregon's state flower, the Oregon Grape. Those, too, were sent back to England and thrive there today as a result of his efforts.

The Reverend Marcus Whitman and wife Narcissa came west in 1836 with the Reverend Henry H. Spalding, his wife Eliza, and seven others, but they left their wagon and buggy at Fort Hall and Fort Boise respectively, as the terrain beyond was perceived as too rough to make the journey with vehicles. In 1838, the Methodists established the first Oregon mission east of the Cascades, which would later become Camp Drum and even later, Fort Dalles. Its location was known to the Indians as Wascopum. At the time, the mission was the white man's only presence in what would later become Wasco County, although Hudson's Bay men would occasionally pass through the area. The same year the Methodist Mission was begun, the Whitman Mission got fully underway near Walla Walla. Their mission at the time was part of Oregon Country, but it later became part of Washington Territory.

The first small waves of immigrants came through the Columbia Gorge in 1841 and 1842, about 111 and 113 in number respectively. The 1841 party of 26 wagons was led by Joseph Meek and the 1842 caravan of 30 wagons by L.W. Hastings. These were the first wagon trains to make it past Walla Walla. Most were men traveling without their families, either to gauge the situation or settle a tract of land and establish a home in the Willamette Valley. The vast majority who arrived in 1842 were unmarried or went back to get their families the following year. The area east of the Cascades was not yet open to settlement, so all but a very few extremely hardy souls continued on to the Willamette Valley west of the Cascades, save for those who forted up for the winter at the mission

The old guard house at Fort Dalles. Note the stone foundation and the plaster and lath interior wall showing through. The building was later used by various parties for a number of purposes, including as a stable. Photo courtesy of The Dalles Chronicle.

at The Dalles because they had arrived too late in the autumn to journey beyond the mountain range.

The "Great Migration" finally began in earnest in 1843, with a multi-part wagon train of about 250 wagons and 900 people, captained by Peter H. Burnett. Orderly Sergeant J.W. Nesmith was the person charged with the difficult task of keeping track of all the people in the train. The group originated in Burnett's home neighborhood of Platte City, Missouri and included women and families. One of the travelers was Nineveh Ford, whose great-great grandson, Cecil Houk, generously shared his research with the author. Mr. Ford's recollections of his Oregon Trail passage were recorded during an interview in Salem on June 17, 1878. Details of his narrative are confirmed in journals kept by other 1843 emigrants.

> I was born in North Carolina on July 15th 1815. Emigrated to Missouri in 1840, and from Missouri to Oregon in 1843. My attention was directed to Oregon by reading Lewis and Clark's journal. The scenery described in that took my fancy; and a desire to see that and to explore the country and return home to North Carolina in 3 years induced me to start. From information from traders and trappers I was confirmed in my intentions. [Note: Although he does not mention him, Nineveh's

Wagon ruts of the Oregon Trail are still visible in several places throughout eastern Oregon, including these just outside Arlington. Photo by Marlene Pointer.

younger brother Ephraim Ford made this crossing with him. Ephraim settled in Yamhill County about 3 miles South of McMinnville.]

In the spring of 1843 Peter H. Burnett of Platte County, Missouri and other prominent men were making up a company to go to Oregon. It was in my neighborhood in Platte City. I was acquainted with the parties. There was another object: One grand objective we had was the prospect of obtaining a donation of land if the country was worth staying in.

At Whitman's station we stopped only a few days. We went immediately on down the Columbia River. We were 6 months on the road from Platte City to Oregon City. Part of the emigration made canoes on the Walla Walla River above Wallula.

I was with the wagons. My wagon was in front of the caravan when it got to The Dalles. The first wagon that landed at The Dalles. There the country would not admit any further travel by wagon. The Cascade Mountains separated us from Willamette Valley. Several of us went into the pine forest there and got dry pine trees and hauled them to the river with our oxen and made rafts of logs; six or eight, one foot to 18 inches diameter, and 20 feet long lashed together. We took our wagons apart and put the bodies on first and put the running gear on the top pieces and the baggage and stuff on top of that and lashed it on.

It becomes clear where the confusion originated regarding the actual end of the Oregon Trail. When the first pioneers came to The Dalles in wagons, for all practical purposes it was the end of the overland journey, as no path over the Cascade mountains existed at the time. An addition to the overland part of the trail would be created three years after the first wagons arrived, thus the Oregon Trail would then extend to Oregon City.

At this point, Ford's group spent two weeks building a short portage road enabling wagon travel around the "cascades"—the river's rapids clearly not navigable in any craft. The Cascade mountain range was named in honor of this challenging part of the Columbia.

Traveling downriver west of the rapids, however, proved to be one of the most difficult segments of the entire Oregon Trail. The Hudson's Bay men had devised a method of rafting small groups down the river with the aid of friendly Indians, using a type of flat-bottomed boat known to the Frenchmen as a bateau. Slightly larger groups were ferried using an innovative log raft able to carry six wagon boxes at a time. These services were offered to immigrant groups by the Frenchmen for a fee. Steamboats and sailboats later traversed the river from its mouth up to the rapids, once the flow of immigrants grew large enough to make it a profitable venture for captains.

Many migrant families could not afford to pay, having traded all but a few material possessions for food or blankets during the final half of the journey. Some had long since spent whatever cash they had brought with them, and it was of little value anyway without a bank anywhere in the territory. Other immigrants simply did not believe the Columbia was any more treacherous than any other river, so they stubbornly refused to pay someone to take them down below the rapids. Whatever their reasons for using the more hazardous method, they would have to raft a number of whirlpools and other hazards in wagon boxes, without benefit of an experienced Native American or Hudson's Bay employee as a pilot.

Making a wagon box function as a raft wasn't extremely difficult, as trail wagons had been designed with this need in mind. The tongue, wheels, and canvas cover were removed, all joints caulked with tallow and tar, and away it went much as Ford described. The difficulty was in navigating the Columbia's treacherous rapids without either smashing the raft to splinters on boulders hidden just beneath the water's surface, or having it thrown ungraciously into a basalt canyon wall after a wild spin through a whirlpool. Many immigrants lost their lives in those rapids during the early years.

Some would reserve one of their wagon boxes with the cover still on for women and children to ride in as a cabin of sorts. On one of the rafts carrying parties from Nineveh Ford's train, there was such a wagon box outfitted to shelter a family. One of the women confined therein delivered a child en route to Oregon City, without the crew aware of the situation until after the child was delivered. According to Mr. Ford, "It was to their great surprise that they heard the cry of an infant."

One of Ford's cousins who had come west on horseback the previous year would meet his party at the other end of the new portage road, providing transport the rest of the way in his boat, *The Peacock*. But Ninevah Ford was too much a gentleman, even in those circumstances, to enjoy the comparative ease of the ride. A group of women and children were transported in the boat and Ford fashioned an interesting craft for his personal transport. His story continues:

I had made my calculation to buy Indian canoes below the Cascades. I succeeded in doing that and my cousin brought the boat and as many as could get in the boat went down. I made a raft of 4 canoes lashing them side by side, taking the wagon beds of 5 wagons to pieces making a platform on top of the canoes, and then taking the running gear apart and putting them on top of the platform; and the baggage on top of the running gears. I lashed it all on securely and hoisted a mast in the center of the craft with a wagon sheet for a sail.

With two Indians and two white men besides myself we set sail for Vancouver. Those were the first wagons brought down the river below the Cascades. It attracted a great deal of attention from the emigrants and others at the time—my fixing such a raft. Some thought it would not bear the trip with 5 wagons and their load of passengers. I had confidence in myself, and I managed the thing myself, and we sailed quite successfully down to Vancouver. They saw the sail. It seemed to them a very odd craft on the river, and they could not distinguish what kind of craft it was. It was not a canoe; it was not a bateau; and they were satisfied it was not a Man of War because they could not see any guns—so they told us after we landed. Many comical remarks were made about the craft when we landed. Dr. McLaughlin [sic] the chief factor at Vancouver was on the shore with quite a company of persons that saw the craft coming. Some 75 or 100 persons of the Hudson Bay Co. and round about came to the shore to see our craft landing.

Then we sailed down the Columbia to the mouth of the Willamette. After we got into the Willamette there came a gale of strong wind up the river in the direction we were going and that endangered our craft; it finally raised the waves six feet high and they would slush over the entire craft and cargo and over our heads. It required two Indians and two white men to bail out the canoes, a man to each canoe. They found that they could bail it out as fast as it would slush in. I kept the craft as near in the middle of the river as possible because it was smoother there than it was near the shore. Our craft ran very rapidly up the stream until we got to the rapids below Oregon City. There the wind slacked up and we tied up for the night. In the morning we towed the craft over the rapids with ropes, 4 men and myself, and we got to Oregon City. It was the first cargo of wagons that ever was landed at Oregon City by land or sea. They were landed on the 10th day of November 1843.

The following account of one incident on that same trip across the plains was authored by Charlotte Matheny Kirkwood in her memoirs. Charlotte's views of pioneer life have been captured in her own colorful language and were compiled in a private memoir, *Into the Eye of the Setting Sun*. Her writings will be distributed throughout this book as appropriate. Used with permission of Walt Davies.

You will note that Mr. Ford conveniently left this part out of his story about the crossing (edited for clarity):

Somewhere near the crossing of the North Platte, we camped at a place called Soap Springs. It was a boggy place. Old Mr. Mills stepped into a sink hole and, as he said: 'went in up to his hat band.' Nineveh Ford's big black ox blundered into one during the night. In the morning he was found and pulled out before Nineveh was up. He was covered, all but his head, with the thick blue mud. Nineveh made a great fuss when he could not find his big black ox.

Everyone else 'hooked up.' There was a lone blue ox grazing about that no one seemed to claim. Nineveh was asked if it were not his. He said, 'No my ox is black.' Finally he was advised to take it anyway, the owner perhaps had yoked up the black ox by mistake. There seemed nothing else to do, so Nineveh, mad as a hornet, went out to catch the ox, while everyone looked on and laughed. After a while Nineveh laughed about it too, but he did not at first. He was still too mad at the man that he thought had taken his big black ox.

Looking out onto Celilo Falls from a fishing platform on the Washington side one can easily see why this part of the Columbia was not navigable. Ben Maxwell, photographer. Oregon Historic Photo Collection, Salem Public Library.

According to records located to date, three wagon trains arrived in 1844, comprised of about 210 wagons and 1,100 people. They were headed by Nathan Ford, Cornelius Gilliam, and Meyer Thorp. A total of 1,765 people (289 wagons) arrived in the six wagon trains crossing The Plains bound for Oregon in 1845. One of those wagons held the family of Samuel Kimbrough Barlow. He and his wife Susannah Lee had married in Indiana in 1820 and had five children with them on the Trail: William, John L., James K., Elizabeth Jane, and Sarah.

Not satisfied with the hazards of rafting down the Columbia, Barlow suggested to his traveling companions that they find a way around the south side of Mount Hood and over the Cascades. The party voted in agreement and the Oregon Trail was destined for change.

On December 9, 1845, Barlow and his brother petitioned Oregon's provisional government at Oregon City for a charter to construct a wagon road over the Cascades. In Barlow's own words, he wanted to build a wagon road from "the dalls Mission to valley of Clackamas."

The bill passed by a margin of eight to two after its required three readings in the Provisional Legislature. It was signed into law on December 18, 1845 and authorized the following tolls as reported in the August 6, 1846 issue of the *Oregon Spectator*: wagons, $5; each head of horses, mules or asses, whether loose,

A huge hollow stump used as a two-horse barn at Parkdale. The creativity of those early settlers was nothing short of amazing. Courtesy of Hood River County Historical Museum.

geared or saddled, 10¢; and each head of horned cattle, whether geared or loose, 10¢.

Sam Barlow and Phillip Foster of Eagle Creek partnered in the venture, with John Ramage providing the bond. Work commenced beginning at Foster's property as soon as weather permitted in the spring of 1846, with a crew of men and oxen providing the labor. Although the road was authorized by the legislature as "Mt. Hood Road," the name never stuck and was always known as the Barlow Road.

One of the more interesting human aspects of those early years was the effect migration had on the love lives of the immigrants, as well as on those they left behind. Many a romance was abandoned in the Midwest in favor of wanderlust. Likewise, many a marriage proposal was made without warning and weddings were hastily performed in unprecedented numbers each spring before the wagon trains departed. The sheer volume of the West's open spaces prompted a loneliness never known before by single men. If single going across the plains, a man would surely be looking for a wife by the time he reached Oregon.

Since many more available men came west each year than women, a father whose family included daughters above the age of 12 was a valuable person for a single fellow to befriend in Oregon country. It was not uncommon for a fully grown man to choose his friend's 13-year-old daughter for his bride without her knowledge. By the time she reached the "marriageable age" of say 14 or 15, her suitor would have worked his way into her life in a variety of subtle—or sometimes not so subtle—ways. If he was wise, he made his intentions clear to the girl and her father virtually the moment she was old enough for courting. A new immigrant male was wise to check into the silent alliances prior to asking a girl to a social function, lest he might unwittingly find himself in a love triangle.

One thing was for certain: although women were in short supply on the western frontier, they weren't able to be the least bit frilly or "lady-like" in their day-to-day activities. No regular freight runs were coming to the Willamette Valley, supplies were in great demand, and the order of the day was to keep things practical. Contrary to "Little House on the Prairie" images, the ladies were not wearing pretty linen dresses and tidy little bonnets. Their dresses were tattered, shoes long since worn through, and underwear was virtually nonexistent. So when a supply run was made, particularly at the end of a good growing season, the man's return generated a great deal of excitement at home. Another of Charlotte Matheny Kirkwood's observations describes this poignant story from the viewpoint of an adolescent girl in 1845:

> In the spring . . . Father and the boys took the boat to Oregon City. They were gone about ten days. Father left the boat at some point a few miles down river and came on home afoot, everyone was excited over his account of what the boat was bringing to us. There was something for all of us, and of course sugar, salt and syrup etc. I was not particularly interested in anything but the wonderful, blue calico dress.

I knew that it was beautiful for hadn't Father, himself, selected it? I asked him over and over to describe it to me, blue with a little yellow figure, he said it was. It was the first new thing I had had since Mrs. Burnett had given me the apron and it was pitifully patched and even the patches were ragged.

The boat was expected in sometime during the next day. I could not sleep that night for thinking about the new dress and I was at the river by day break to watch for it. It seemed a long time in coming. It was hours, even after the boat came in sight, for the river was very swift over the bar. At last they tied up to the bank and all the family was there to see the unloading. The packages were handed out and unwrapped.

Mary's dress came first. I was usually pleased to see others happy, I wasn't then. I was dead to every emotion save anticipation of my own wonderful dress, blue and yellow and I loved both. Mother's dress was unpacked, anyone at all could see by looking at her that she needed one quite as badly as I did. There were things for everyone, even the Indian boys were not overlooked. I was impatient. I think Father hurried, but it seemed to take a long while, finally the last bundle was undone, it was something of brother Adam's. The tragedy stunned me, my dress was gone. I never cried, but a great smothering lump came into my throat. I can still see the tears in my Father's eyes, big and tender and blue they were swimming in them. I do not remember that anything was said to me, it was one of those things that words could not help. I went off by myself to fight it out.

No one ever knew what became of my dress, either it was lost out of the boat, tho everything else was there, or what was more likely, the store keeper had failed to put it in. Poor Father, it hurt him terribly, he was always so tender toward me.

For months I used to wander up and down the river banks and dream about my dress and try to picture what it would have looked like.

3. WAGONS HO!
IN THEIR OWN WORDS

As the Indians saw more whites making their way to the Willamette Valley each year, they became restless, fearing that the white man would force tribes to give up long-held properties and natural resources. As it turned out, they were not overreacting.

Although most tribes had grown to have a basic trust in the missionaries and many other whites, it was built on an unstable foundation. Even the strongest ties between Native and white were tested by circumstances neither could control. Such was the case when the white men's diseases began to follow them into Indian country. The late November 1847 massacre of the Whitman family at the Waiilatpu mission near Walla Walla was a result of the measles epidemic. As the Cayuse Indian population began to fall ill and die, tribesmen felt their trust had been betrayed and the Whitman party had intentionally brought evil upon them.

Operating under the assumption that Dr. and Mrs. Whitman were part of a larger conspiracy to kill off the native population and gain control of the land, many of the Cayuse tribe were not willing to believe Whitman's explanation of the measles epidemic. Chiefs Tiloukaikt (also spelled Teloquoit, Teloquit, and Telakite in official documents) and Tamahas planned to attack the Whitman party in the most unlikely setting: in broad daylight, inside their home, and during a visit that seemed like any other. Although their pre-attack behavior alerted some household members that something was amiss, precautions were not taken until it was too late. Dr. Whitman was away from the house, just returning when his wife realized their fate was sealed. As the good doctor entered his home, he was shot to death in front of Mrs. Whitman and several children. Others who lived at the mission, including women and older children, were also killed in the following hours. Mrs. Whitman was included among the ranks of the dead.

When word of the massacre reached Oregon City nine days later, it was evident the situation with the Cayuse tribe must be brought under control immediately if there was any hope of assuring that other tribes in the area didn't follow suit. The Oregon Provisional Legislature was in session at the time and took immediate action to gather troops and secure the mission at The Dalles. Rumors and speculation fueled the fires of fear and soon they were planning an all-out war on the native population, as they initially thought the Hudson's Bay men were united with the Indians in a cooperative effort to win Oregon Territory for benefit of the British crown.

Due to the distance between the Oregon Territory and "the States," it would not be possible for them to gain assistance from the regular military units of the Army. Local volunteer troops needed to be raised and they would also need to supply their own horses, clothing, guns, and ammunition. The governor was authorized to raise a regiment of 500 men led by Colonel Cornelius Gilliam, Lieutenant-Colonel James Waters, and Major H.A. J. Lee. The first 45 men were assembled that afternoon, to be called the "Oregon Rifles." A march was led from there to Vancouver, down the north bank of the Columbia, and across the river above the rapids. It took them five days to reach The Dalles.

Several battles ensued, beginning with multiple skirmishes at The Dalles beginning immediately upon the regiment's arrival. Messengers had been dispatched from Oregon City to all settlements west of the Cascades, where they gathered volunteers, but it would be several weeks before a full regiment would arrive in The Dalles. The small band of volunteers continued to defend the mission until around February 1, 1848, when the full regiment arrived. Gilliam, Waters, and Lee formed three companies totalling 537 men. One company would remain at the mission and patrol the area, while others were dispatched to Walla Walla and encountered hostile tribes along the way.

The first battle outside the immediate area of The Dalles was fought on a steep ridge bordering a tribal village near the Deschutes River in central Oregon. Colonel Gilliam's philosophy was that it was better to fight the enemy in only one direction at a time, so his troops were taken to every possible location between central Oregon and the Walla Walla valley to show their strength in hopes of discouraging other tribes from participating. What he didn't want was to be fighting a band of Indians in front of the troops and discover another band behind them. The few tribesmen near the Deschutes scattered upon a minimal show of firepower, just as Gilliam had hoped.

His troops checked the village to see if the warriors had fled there, but discovered the village had been deserted. When asked by one of his troops if they should take the food stores for themselves and burn the village, the colonel showed his true colors. Although his troops were without food due to a late provision transport, he said, "No, I can fight the bucks; but I cannot fight the helpless women and children. It is now winter; and if you burn their village they will likely perish. Let us leave it just as we found it; and it may have a good effect." Gilliam and his men lived on horse meat for the next two days, until the provisions wagon caught up with them. They then headed north and east toward Cayuse country.

Near Butter Creek, Gilliam's soldiers met up with a large band of Native Americans whose numbers were enough to make any man doubt his ability to survive what lay ahead. Gilliam, sensing the doubt of his men, gave them this piece of advice:

> Boys, the murderers of Doctor Whitman are before us with their allies;
> and behind them on the hill are as many more ready to join them in case

Native American in his dugout canoe, Celilo Photo by Ben Gifford, courtesy of Hood River County Historical Museum.

the battle goes against us. You know the consequence if we fail; not one of us will be left to tell the tale. And that is not the worst. Every tribe of Indians in the whole country will unite to desolate our homes and to exterminate and drive all the Americans from this county. But we are not going to fail. We are going to whip them and teach them a lesson to-day that they will never forget. Don't shoot until you are ordered. Obey your officers, and quietly wait until you are ordered to begin the battle.

The Indians gauged a well-planned battle against the troops, advancing toward them slowly at first and encircling Gilliam and his men in a perfect procession. When the circle of warriors was two men deep, they attacked swiftly. In a sudden flash of recognition, Lieutenant Charles McKay yelled: "Colonel, I know that Indian. He is their great medicine man, and their leader here. He has made those Indians believe we cannot kill him, that our balls cannot harm or penetrate him. Let me shoot him. I believe I can kill him." "Kill him," replied Colonel Gilliam; and at the crack of the gun the medicine man fell from his horse. This so upset the warriors that they lost their rhythm and, seemingly, their cause. Their disarray allowed Gilliam's troops to extricate themselves and move to an offensive position. Still reeling from the loss of their supposedly invincible medicine man, the warriors pursued them in a half-hearted series of skirmishes throughout the day, but made no further attacks.

After the Native Americans departed late in the afternoon, Gilliam's men gathered the seriously wounded troops on makeshift gurneys and a group of men carried them toward Walla Walla; Colonel Waters was included among the

Early Fort Dalles. Photo courtesy of The Dalles Chronicle.

injured. The following morning, as the troops set out for Walla Walla, they were met by a small group of Indians carrying white flags. The warriors asked for a suspension of hostilities and a proposal to meet with the officers to attempt a peace talk. Colonel Gilliam opposed the idea, thinking it to be a ruse enabling the entire band of Cayuse Indians to escape from the area. He had been assigned on-site army commissioners, however, and they insisted he seize the opportunity for a peaceful settlement. The peace talk was set for the following morning.

As Gilliam and his officers set out for the peace meeting the next morning, they saw clouds of dust emanating from the nearby mountainside. The entire village had fled to the safety of the Palouse tribe east of the Blue Mountains. The troops had been duped. They would stop at Waiilatpu and bury the victims of the massacre in a mass grave and set up a makeshift hospital for the wounded soldiers at the mission.

From there, the remaining troops continued east, into Palouse country, in an attempt to dissuade the Palouse and other tribes from offering asylum to the exiled Cayuse tribe or joining them against the white population. Gilliam hoped to convince the Cayuse to turn Whitman's murderers over to them for prosecution. A couple of hard chases ensued as the soldiers attempted to round up the murderers, and dozens of Gilliam's men were lost in battle. As the colonel joined the segment of his troops dispatched to make the long trip back to Fort Dalles to meet the supply wagons, they stopped for the night near Well's Springs. It was his intent to meet with the governor in person at The Dalles to discuss a strategy for bringing the Yakima War to a close.

It was Gilliam's custom to tend his own horse, so he went over to unburden it for the night's rest. Finding the steed's rope entangled with others, he struggled to untangle them. One of his men was cleaning his rifle nearby and noticed

Gilliam's frustration, and went over to offer his help. As the soldier bent down to reach for the rope, his gun accidentaly discharged with the cleaning rod still in the barrel. The rod penetrated Gilliam's skull so quickly and efficiently that he was killed instantly. The impact of the blow knocked him flat on his back, arms straight out to the sides, with his eyes closed, according to one source, "looking as natural as life but for the rod protruding from his head." Despite surviving numerous battles in recent months, he lost his life in a freak accident at the end of a long day.

Colonel Waters and Lieutenant-Colonel Lee were still in Palouse country, of what is now north Idaho and eastern Washington, with their troops when they received word of Gilliam's death. Although they proceeded as far north as Spokane, they were not able to locate the band of Indians harboring the fugitives who committed the Whitman massacre. The band had gone to Montana, so the troops returned to The Dalles without further incident, and the Cayuse War was over. Much later, a small group of the offending parties was brought by their own tribesmen to Fort Vancouver to atone for the attack at Waiilatpu.

The Methodist Mission at The Dalles was officially closed in 1848 due to the unrest between the Indians and pioneers. In late summer of 1848, the First Regiment Oregon Mounted Rifles arrived at Vancouver, the first regular Army troops to be stationed in the Oregon Territory. Several of the men who volunteered for the Oregon Rifles or came west with them chose to settle east of the Cascades as a result of the impressions they formed while stationed in The Dalles. The Mounted Rifles assumed a peacekeeping role with the Native Americans after their arrival, and things stayed fairly quiet for the next few years.

Amidst all the conflict, pioneer families needed to keep their focus on long-term objectives. Life went on and progress was made, despite the nearly constant interruptions for military or civic service. Within a couple of years after arriving, most families were growing prolific gardens and enough grain to supply their own families. As we see in the following narrative, even an adolescent girl could appreciate the advantages—as well as some of the disadvantages—of living in this new country. Again, we can experience pioneer life in the eyes of Charlotte Matheny Kirkwood (excerpted from her "Harvest Time" story):

After the first two or three years, the early settlers could have plenty, not a great variety, it is true, but enough to keep real hunger away. That is, of course, if they were wise enough to look ahead. We always had plenty, but I was sick and I craved dainty things and the coarse fare was not palatable to me, bacon, dried peas, coarse flour, bread and such like. We always had plenty of money, but there was nothing to buy. It was not until after the gold mines were discovered that sail vessels came to our coast to bring sugar and tea and other things that were luxuries.

In the fall when the grain was ripe, it was cut by hand. Ten or a dozen men, each taking a swath as wide as he could reach with the swing of the scythe and around and around the field they would go. A cradle attached

33

to the blade of the scythe held the loose, long straw to be dropped in a windrow at the outer edge of the swath with each stroke of the long blade. Behind the cradlers came the men who raked the straw into piles as large as would make a good sized bundle. Then the bundlers, catching up a handful of straw, would twist and fashion it into a band, then catching up the pile of straw a twist and a final tuck and the bundle was ready to be shocked into groups of five or six, the heads of grain turned up to the sun.

Farmers helped each other with the threshing as well as the cutting of the grain and sometimes it was well into the winter before everyone's grain would be stored away in sacks or bins. A few days before threshing was to start, the farmers would round up their wild horses. When everything was ready at the farm where the work was to begin, 40 or 50 of the wild horses would be driven there and corralled in a pen that opened to the threshing floor.

Our threshing floor was not really a floor at all, but just a smooth, level bit of hard ground with a high wall around it. Gates opened from it to a couple of corrals. The wild horses were driven into one of these pens and kept there till the floor had been covered to a depth of three or four feet with the loose bundles of grain. Then 15 or 20 of the horses would be driven onto it. They were exactly as wild as antelopes. The

Menefee block house: one of the few local blockhouses that survived long enough to be captured on film in later years. Courtesy of The Dalles Chronicle.

loose straw under foot and men and boys hollering and waving their hats, frightened the imprisoned animals into the wildest panic. Back and forth and round and round they would plunge. When their speed would slacken, men with long whips would urge them on and on till flakes of foam and sweat would drip from their flanks. Then they would be turned into the empty corral and men would go onto the threshing floor and turn the straw, or if the grain had been shattered easily, the straw would be thrown out and new bundles would be spread on the floor and fresh horses would be turned in. The threshing at each farm might last for a week or two. It was a wonderful time for us children. The men, themselves, seemed to enjoy it.

And so the threshing would go on at each farm in its turn till it was all done. Then the herd of jaded and now thoroughly broken horses would be divided and taken home to be ridden or worked by their owners.

But that did not finish the harvest. At our house there would be maybe a thousand bushels of grain on the threshing floor and as many bushels, or more of chaff and broken straw. Separating the grain from the chaff was a tedious task. It was usually done by the farmers themselves.

A high platform would be built in a place well exposed to the wind. Sacks of the grain would be carried up to a man who stood on the platform, then he would pour it slowly into the sweep of the wind. The heavier grain falling neat and clean in a pile at the base of the platform, while the lighter straw and chaff, would scatter and carry away. The grain that was to be used for seed or flour would be run through the fanning mill. Oh! how I hated that fanning mill. I am not sure, but I think I would be afraid of it even yet. I used to have to keep the cleaned grain cleared away from the front of it and I would rather have faced wild horses. I do not really know why I was afraid of it, but I was. It stood in the grainary and I never went there unless I was sent for something.

Things were getting easier for us and Mother seemed quite happy and contented. It is true that there were not a great many people in the country even then [barely more than 4,000 in all of Oregon country], it was a time in November of 1847 that I have in mind, but several families that we liked and neighbored with were near us and told us of things that were happening in other parts of our new country. Our lives had settled into the new ways and we were contented and happy in a peaceful valley.

Progress toward settlement continued, and in 1848 Oregon received territorial status. In 1850, the Army officially opened Camp Drum, whose name was later changed to Fort Dalles. Up to that point, the area now known as The Dalles was generally referred to as "Dalles," which was the French word used by Hudson's Bay men to describe that part of the Columbia River—"the trough."

The United States Mail route was extended north and westward as far as The Dalles in 1851, mostly as a result of the increase in ship traffic between Oregon and California during the gold rush. Prior to that time, much unofficial mail was moved to and from loved ones by emigrants going west and explorers returning to their eastern homes. It was not uncommon to see a letter addressed to someone in Oregon, but it traveled as regular mail only as far as Salt Lake City, Utah, or San Francisco, California. It might sit for weeks or even months in those more developed locations until a ship captain or other potential courier was kind enough to transport a bag of mail on his next run to Oregon country.

By the end of 1849, just over 11,000 immigrants had arrived in the Willamette Valley, most by way of the Gorge, and the east side of the Cascades was still not officially open to settlement. Major G.J. Raines of the Army post at The Dalles reported a total of just 35 permanent white settlers between the Cascades and the Rockies during the winter of 1853–1854.

Many men went to California during the gold rush when it began in 1849 and, having investigated Oregon on their way home from the mines, returned to the east just long enough to load their families into wagons and head for Oregon. 1852–1854 brought increased immigration: as many as 3,000 to 4,000 people traveled through the Gorge each year en route to the Willamette Valley.

The 1850 Donation Land Claim (DLC) act added fuel to the immigration fires, granting 320 acres to each white male over the age of 21. Furthermore, as acknowledgement of the importance of extraordinary work done by women on the western frontier, the territorial government sweetened the pot with an additional 320 acres to be granted to every married woman when her husband received his claim. A woman was given title to her 320 acres in her own name, an unprecedented gift from the government in that day. Widows who otherwise fit the DLC criteria were also granted land, but single women did not qualify.

As one might expect, this extra gift was additional incentive for a single man to take a wife as soon as possible after he arrived on the frontier. A typical early settler couple took out a claim for their 640 acres in the Willamette Valley and proved it up as quickly as possible. Those who relocated in the 1860s and 1870s then sold their DLC property to a later settler and used the money to purchase property east of the Cascades. Unfortunately, this is where wives usually came up short on the deal, as the new property was often purchased in the husband's name alone. Since only the earliest settlers qualified for the DLCs, only a small percentage of them were used directly to obtain land east of the Cascades.

Mrs. Cook made the trip with her family in 1852 and later married Amos Cook. Amos was one of the earliest pioneers to travel through the Columbia Gorge, which he did with pack horses in 1840. Some of Cook's offspring resided in The Dalles and other Gorge communities. Readers may also recognize the name of Abigail Scott Duniway in this story as a prominent suffragette who pressed for women's rights. Abigail ("Jenny") played a large part in women gaining the right to vote in local elections a number of years after the

Scott family's arrival in Oregon. The following is excerpted from Fred Lockley's column, "Impressions & Observations of the Journal Man" in the *Oregon Daily Journal* on March 21, 1925:

"We came to Oregon in 1852," said Mrs. Mary Frances Scott Cook, at the home of her daughter, Mrs. F.G. Young, "My father, John Tucker Scott, was born February 18, 1809, 18 miles from where Abraham Lincoln was born and six days prior to his birth. When father was 15 he went with his parents to Illinois. He was 43 when we started to Oregon, in 1852. My Mother's maiden name was Ann Roelofson. I was born May 19, 1833, not far from Peoria, in Tazewell county, Illinois. I was the second child and the eldest daughter in a family of 15.

My father was captain of our train of 27 wagons. My mother died of cholera on June 20, about two days' travel, by ox-team, this side of Fort Laramie, or about 30 miles. We buried her wrapped in a blanket in a shallow grave by the side of the road. Father and the others heaped stones over the grave so that the coyotes and other animals might not disturb it. My brother Willie died in the Blue mountains in what is now called Baker county.

We came by way of the Barlow road. That statement means a good deal to a pioneer of Oregon, for he knows what a rough and difficult road it

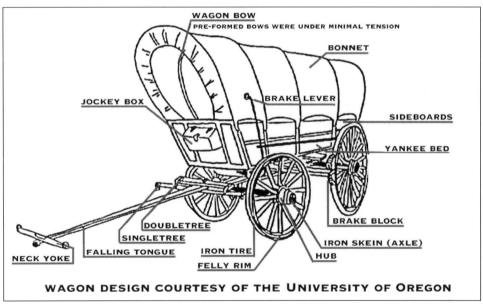

WAGON DESIGN COURTESY OF THE UNIVERSITY OF OREGON

The trail wagon was designed with a shorter box than the Conestoga wagon to lighten the load and make navigation easier over more difficult terrain. Trail wagons were made the size of a standard eastern farm utility wagon—with the addition of a water-tight bonnet and slanted side rails to keep the rain out.

was. After the death of my mother, I had to serve as the mother of the family. We settled at Lafayette [Oregon]. Father ran a hotel there, owned by Amos Cook, called the Temperance house. Among our boarders I remember best Judge M.P. Dealy, Judge Bolse [Bowles] and David Logan. Lafayette was the county seat, and these men came there on legal business. Father ran the hotel till his girls married. Not being able then to get good help, he went out of the hotel business. My sister Jennie was the first married. We always called her Jennie, though her name was Abigail Jane Scott. She married Mr. Duniway, August 1, 1853. I was married two weeks later to Amos Cook, who came to Oregon in 1840. We were married August 16, 1853, by Rev. Neely Johnson. I moved to my husband's farm, which he had taken up in 1841, and lived there 35 years.

My husband came to Oregon in the party with Francis Fletcher. They arrived in the spring of 1840. They procured seed wheat of Dr. McLoughlin; also a barrel of molasses. They used boiled wheat in place of bread, and ate molasses on it. In those days you did not have to leave your place to kill a deer, game was so abundant. My husband put in six months or so working at the Methodist Mission, near Wheatland, while his partner ran both of the places.

James A. Hurst, about 10 years after he (age 20) and his wife Malinda (age 16) crossed the plains in 1851. Their son Joseph was born about six weeks after they arrived in Oregon. Courtesy of the Hurst family archives.

They had a pretty hard trip across the plains. We also experienced some hardships crossing. At Fort Hall my shoes had become completely worn out, so I went barefoot. Our cattle were worn and thin. There was a large family of us, so we older children walked. My feet became cracked. It was impossible to walk without occasionally stepping on the spines of the prickly pear, and when they broke off in your feet they had to fester out. By the time we came to Laurel hill our food was exhausted. For two days all any of us had to eat was salal berries.

You will find if you try it that salal berries are not very strengthening to walk on or to work on. After our two days' diet of salal berries, we met a man who had some moldy flour. He let us have some of it and we camped right there and baked bread. Some relatives (Neill Johnson) came out from French Prairie to meet us with two yoke of oxen and plenty of flour and meat. I don't have to tell you how glad we were to see them. I carried my sister, who was 5 years old, through the Grand Ronde valley. We had left our home, at Groveland, Ill., early in April, 1852. In our immediate party were my father, John Tucker Scott; my mother, myself, my sisters, Abigail Jane, and Margaret Ann, my brother Harvey, my sisters, Catherine Amanda and Harriet Louise, my brother, John Henry, my sister Sarah Maria and my brother, William Niell."

According to family records, they started from Illinois with 42 oxen, three cows, two horses, and one pony. The three cows died on the plains, one of the horses drowned in Snake River in what is now Idaho, and another wandered off in the Cascades. Only seven of the 42 oxen survived the trip, only slightly worse than the average percentage of losses.

Like others before and after them, they descended the 2-mile drop known as Laurel Hill by felling heavy trees and tying them behind their wagons as a control mechanism. The next day some of their oxen escaped and had to be hunted for, the king bolt of one wagon broke and had to be replaced, and a wagon tongue broke and had to be mended. The combination allowed them to advance only 4 miles, despite the fact they were within about 12 miles of their final destination. They finally reached Oregon City the following day, September 30.

Modern women who are tempted to pamper themselves during a pregnancy or after giving birth might want to consider what the pioneer women experienced on their six-month journey across the plains. Since migrating was primarily a youthful pursuit, especially in the earliest years, many first-time mothers gave birth immediately before the trip or somewhere along the way.

Malinda Davis Hurst had no idea she was pregnant when she and her husband James departed Missouri in April of 1851, just five months after their marriage. One can only guess what she thought when she realized, somewhere in Kansas, that her queasy stomach and extreme tiredness were not a result of being on the road. Her voracious appetite probably contributed to the fact that the couple's provisions were exhausted by the time they reached The Dalles. They temporarily

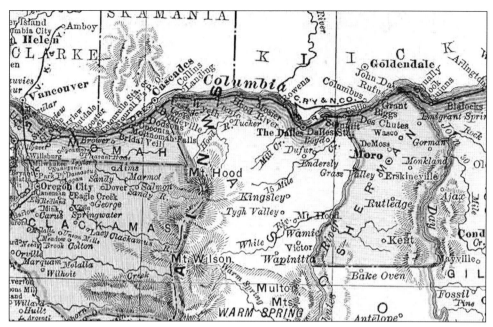

A slice of the 1895 Rand-McNally map, showing the area covered by this book. Not shown: several towns on the Washington side, including White Salmon, Bingen, and Lyle.

parted company so he could take their stock over the Barlow Trail while she rode the wagon as a raft down the Columbia. At that point she made five biscuits out of their last bit of flour. She would have but two biscuits to sustain herself and the unborn infant, and James would have the other three biscuits to last until they met again on the other side of the Cascade mountains a few days later. Generous Dr. John McLoughlin at Fort Vancouver provided Malinda with additional food to sustain the couple until they were settled enough to begin trading. Having walked nearly 2,000 miles during the previous six months, Malinda gave birth to their first child, Joseph, about six weeks after their arrival in Oregon City.

Journals kept by Oregon Trail travelers during the 1850s and oral histories passed down to succeeding generations are illuminating. Most immigrants attempted to keep a sense of humor about their travels, and even those who found little humor in the moment remembered the journey with a bittersweet mixture of humor and stoic realism. Sometimes, mental images painted by their stories lend themselves to humor perceived by the reader where none was intended by the writer. The following is an excerpt from a reminiscence written by Mrs. Frances Hatcher, one of the 1852 Oregon Trail travelers in a different train than a previous story about the Scott family:

> When we left our home we did not intend to stay away but 5 years; nevertheless it was a sad parting from our home and loved ones as we knew it was a long and venturesome trip. We started with three wagons

which were to meet at a certain place on the road. A neighbor man came with a small wagon to take Mrs. Knifong, her three children, myself and children to where the wagons were. We were each at our mother's home. How well I remember when I bid my mother goodbye and we waved at each other as far as we could see. Mrs. Knifong was in the wagon crying when they came by for me. She had a short time before she told her mother goodbye. We both cried, going about a mile before we spoke to each other and then I said brokenly, "It is awful hard to part with a mother." and then she answered bursting into tears again, "It is hard."

My second day's experience was when we crossed Medicine Creek, Missouri. The creek was pretty deep to ford. The men thought the women had better ride behind them on horseback. I rode behind a young man with my baby Columbus in his arms. When we crossed over, the horse got in the mud, foundered and threw me off in the water. The man threw the baby on one side and he jumped off the other. I got out of the water, ran and picked up my baby, went up the hill, all dripping with mud and water. They all laughed at me and I told them after this, I was going to stick to the wagon.

But there was also a gravely serious side to the journals, as is evident in these excerpts taken from the 1852 journal kept by James Akin, Jr.:

Our little sister, Mary Ann Akin, died at the Cascades and was buried there. We were at the Cascades about a week waiting for the steamboat to bring us down to Portland. Our father died two weeks after we reached Portland.

By this time, larger watercraft offered yet another option to those who could afford to pay for passage down the Columbia River below the rapids and had sufficient provisions to last an extra week. The family of Walter McFarland was one of many that lacked funding to go down the Columbia by steamer or other large vessel. Here is a short excerpt from Sarah Sprenger McFarland's 1852 trail recollection:

Some of the [McFarland] brothers took the big wagon over the Cascade Mountains. The rest of us took a flat boat to the Cascades, from where we went around the cascades [referring to the rapids, not the mountains] in the wagon to the lower Columbia River. There we took a flat boat again to Sandy River, quite a way below Oregon City. At that point our brothers met us with the big wagon and we started together for Oregon City.

On our way down the Columbia, the wind started to blow so hard that we had to put ashore. It happened to be on a pretty steep place, but we had to stay there all night nevertheless. How we managed to sleep and eat our food without slipping is more than I can tell.

Although a relatively small number of people had crossed the plains to Oregon during the first decade of emigration, those who had crossed made every effort to encourage others to come west every year. They nearly had the packing list down to a science. Advice given in the *Emigrant's Guide to Oregon and California*, first published in 1845, included the following:

> Travel in companies of 40 to 50 wagons and continue together the whole route, don't race your oxen.
>
> LOADING & SUPPLIES
> The loading of the wagons should consist mostly of provisions. Do not burden yourselves with furniture or many beds. Bring a few light trunks or very light boxes to pack clothes in. No heavy articles except a few cooking vessels, coal shovel, pair of pot hooks, water keg, tin canister to hold milk, a few tin cups, tin plates, tin saucers, butcher knifes, and one small grindstone in the company.
>
> CLOTHING & BEDDING
> Bring clothes enough to last one year, including several pair of strong, heavy shoes to each person. Bring but few bedclothes, for they will wear out by the time you arrive here. Blankets can be purchased here or exchanged for labor or commodities.

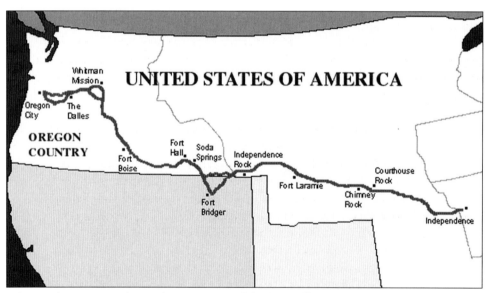

The grueling 1,900-plus mile Oregon Trail had its official beginning at Independence, Missouri, and ended at Oregon City. The loop in the Trail at The Dalles represents the difficult choice early travelers made between rafting the Columbia River or taking their wagons behind Mount Hood via Barlow Road.

GUNS & AMMUNITION
You will need rifles, shotguns, pistols, 6 pounds powder, 12 pounds lead for each man and shot. For killing buffalo the best size bore for a rifle is 40 to the pound, but a smaller calibre will be better suited for game west of the mountains. Large flintlock guns are good to traffic with the Snake Indians.

TRADING GOODS
Bring plenty of cheap cotton shirts to trade with the Indians. Also bring blankets, red and blue cloth, tobacco, butcher knives, fish hooks, flints, lead, powder, beads, bells, rings, mirrors and rice.

A typical day on the Oregon Trail might include travel over anywhere from 8 to 12 miles. Some parts were so rough that it was impossible to cover more than 5 or 6 miles, but desert travel necessitated as many as 20 or more miles in a single day, due to lack of water. Water and good grass for grazing were the inspiration for each day's goals. The emigrants also hoped to find enough wood lying around at the next camp to provide them with adequate cooking fires that could be enjoyed for warmth in the early mornings as well. Still, the main concern was water, so they frequently had to use dried buffalo chips as cooking fuel. Women and children often walked most of the way to spare the oxen some of the heavy load, so the prospect of scavenging for buffalo chips was not a welcome one when they might otherwise be sitting around the fire.

To gain a better appreciation of the day-to-day travels over the trail, we would need to walk many miles in the emigrants' shoes. To understand how the Columbia Gorge and surrounding area looked to these weary travelers, we need only read this diary entry of 1853 traveler Mrs. Amelia Stewart Knight. Her entourage began its journey in Monroe County, Iowa, on April 9. These are her impressions of all she saw and experienced on her party's crossing over the Barlow Road:

> Tuesday, September 6th—Still in camp, washing and overhauling the wagons to make them as light as possible to cross the mountains. Evening—After throwing away a good many things and burning up most of the deck boards of our wagons so as to lighten them, got my washing and cooking done and started on again. Crossed two [river] branches, traveled 3 miles and have camped near the gate [to the Barlow Road] or foot of the Cascade Mountains (here I was sick all night, caused by my washing and working too hard).
>
> Wednesday, September 7th—First day in the mountains. Came 16 miles today; crossed Deschutes, or a branch of it, 4 times and have encamped on the bank of it. Bought flour at 20 cents per pound to feed the stock.
>
> Thursday, September 8th—Traveled 14 miles over the worst road that was ever made [Barlow Road], up and down, very steep, rough and rocky hills, through mud holes, twisting and winding around stumps,

logs and fallen trees. Now we are on the end of a log, now over a big root of a tree; now bounce down in a mud hole, then bang goes the other side of the wagon, and woe be to whatever is inside. There is very little chance to turn out of this road, on account of timber and fallen trees, for these mountains are a dense forest of pines, fir, white cedar or redwood (the handsomest timber in the world must be here in these Cascade Mountains). Many of the trees are 300 feet high and so dense to almost exclude the light of heaven, and for my own part I dare not look to the top of them for fear of breaking my neck. We have camped on a little stream called Sandy. No feed for the stock except flour, and by driving them a mile or so, they can get a little swamp grass or pick brush.

Friday, September 9th—Came eight and a half miles. Crossed Sandy 4 times; came over corduroy roads, through swamps, over rocks and hummocks, and the worst road that could be imagined or thought of, and have encamped about one o'clock in a little opening near the road. The men have driven the cattle a mile off from the road to try and find grass and rest them till morning. We hear the road is still worse ahead. There is a great deal of laurel growing here, which will poison the stock if they eat it. There is no end to the wagons, buggies, yokes, chains, etc. that are lying all along this road. Some splendid good wagons just left standing, perhaps with the owners' names on them; and many are the poor horses, mules, oxen, cows, etc. that are lying dead in these mountains. Afternoon—Slight shower.

Saturday, September 10th—Pleasant. Noon—We have just halted in a little valley at the foot of Big Laurel Hill to rest ourselves and the poor, weary cattle an hour or so. We dare not rest long in these mountains, for fear of a storm, which would be almost certain to kill all our stock, although the poor things need it bad enough, after what they have gone through with this forenoon. It would be useless for me with my pencil to describe the awful road we have just passed over (let fancy picture a train of wagons and cattle passing through a crooked chimney and we have Big Laurel Hill).

After descending several bad hills, one called Little Laurel Hill, which I thought is as bad as could be, but in reality it was nothing to this last one called Big Laurel. It is something more than half mile long, very rocky all the way, quite steep, winding, sideling, deep down, slippery and muddy, made so by a spring running the entire length of the road, and this road is cut down so deep that at times the cattle and wagons are almost out of sight, with no room for the drivers except on the bank, a very difficult place to drive, also dangerous, and to make the matter worse, there was a slow poking train ahead of us, which kept stopping every few minutes, and another behind us which kept swearing and hurrying our folks on, and there they all were, with the poor cattle all on the strain, holding back the heavy wagons on the slippery road. The men and boys all had their hands full, and I was obliged to take care of myself and little ones as best I could, there being no path or road except the one where the teams traveled. We kept as near the road as we could, winding round the fallen timber and brush, climbing over logs, creeping under fallen timber. To keep from smelling the carrion, I, as others, holding my nose. (Must quit, as all hands are getting ready to travel again.)

Evening—Came 10 miles today. Crossed Sandy River once and have camped by it about dark. Fed the stock flour and cut down alders for them to browse on. Nothing else for them, poor things. Kept them yoked and tied all night (there I was sick all night and not able to get out of the wagon in the morning).

Little wonder it was a difficult choice to make between taking the Barlow Road or risking the wild ride down the Columbia. What a cruel trick it must have seemed to have come so far and endured six months of deprivation, only to find that the most difficult and treacherous part of the journey may still lie between them and their goal.

Commercial fishing in the early days employed whatever means were available. Here the crew includes three men who use a horse and a boat to bring the salmon-filled seine net ashore.

4. More Indian Wars and a Super-sized County

Things were relatively quiet between natives and pioneers for a while after 1848. Conflicts were generally minor and easily controlled by the Army regulars who arrived after the Whitman massacre. More than four years of relative peace ended in the Rogue River Valley of southern Oregon in 1853.

Rather than a conflict concentrated in a single location, the 1853 battle involved a series of tribes scattered throughout the region. It began with the Rogue River tribe of southern Oregon but was seemingly resolved fairly quickly. A treaty was signed between the federal government and representatives of the Rogue River tribe on September 8, 1853, but it was not ratified. No sooner had they signed the treaty than the troops were sent to quell a similar situation taking place with the Yakima tribe in the northern part of the Oregon Territory (now southern Washington state). It, too, was smoothed out in a matter of weeks; two years of relative peace followed.

Meanwhile, on January 11, 1854, Wasco County in the Oregon Territory was created as the largest county in the nation, encompassing 130,000 square miles. It spanned not only the entire Columbia Gorge, but extended from the Cascade Mountains eastward to the Rockies. Nearly all of what is now Idaho, as well as the western edges of both Wyoming and Montana were included in Wasco's boundaries.

With so few settlers between the Cascades and the Rockies, many in the territorial legislature argued that the area was too scarcely populated to warrant formation of a county. It was formed anyway, based on the volume of commercial transactions taking place between the western and eastern parts of the Oregon Territory. By forming a county, the territorial government was able to form a local government that might better manage affairs on the east side of the mountains even before its inevitable settlement.

In the same year, the first settlers arrived at Hood River. Oregon's Territorial Legislature passed laws forbidding the sale of arms, ammunition, and "ardent spirits" to Indians. Another law prohibited "Negroes, mulattoes, and Indians, or persons one half or more of Indian blood" from participating in proceedings involving a white person. These laws were repealed a short time later.

The West became wild once more in September 1855 when Major Gabriel J.

Raines, stationed at Fort Dalles, issued orders to Major Granville O. Haller to gather a company of at least 150 men. About 400 enlisted men under Raines's command were ordered to go into Yakima Indian territory to take punitive measures against the Indians in retaliation for the murder of Indian Agent A.J. Bolin.

Chief Kamaiakin of the Yakima tribe was considered a physical and intellectual giant by many, both within and outside of his tribe. At more than 6 feet tall, his mere physical presence commanded respect, but he was also extremely intelligent. The combination made him powerful. He befriended white men as he felt it appropriate and beneficial, but his concerns about the influx of pioneers had continued to grow rather than diminish with time. His wariness of the white settlers transferred directly to his tribesmen, ultimately leading to a high level of distrust. Bolin's death was the result.

When the original small group of soldiers was dispatched, they were outnumbered about 10 to 1 on the battlefield. Regardless, they fought all day and into the night, then again the next day and night. A messenger was dispatched on the second day to seek reinforcements from Fort Dalles. By the third day they were undoubtedly exhausted from battle. The Indians kept the pressure on by keeping a "running fight" throughout the night, further tiring the already weary soldiers.

About 25 miles outside of Wascopum, the men were met by Lieutenant Day with 45 men of the Third Artillery. Major Haller reported the loss of five soldiers from his company and most of the company's horses and supplies. The Major

A group of Native Americans decked out in full tribal regalia gets together for a pow-wow. They may have been members of the Warm Springs Confederated Tribes gathered for the spring root festival. Courtesy of Barbara Coles.

requested another 1,000 reinforcements, but volunteers were in short supply, and Captain Fitzgerald of The Dalles could only muster 319 more soldiers.

A company of men was assigned to protect Fort Dalles while the others were commanded to press onward toward the Yakima Valley. Troops fought in several skirmishes throughout eastern Washington Territory, frequently assigned to companies that would be dispatched to a distant area, then reconnoiter with the unit as a whole. Rather than quell the uprising of the Yakima tribe, the troops found themselves embroiled in a war much lager than originally envisioned. Bolin's murder was only a symptom of a much larger ailment.

The nearby Klickitat tribe had established very friendly relationships with the few settlers who encroached upon their native lands, so when Chief Kamaiakin encouraged the Klickitats to join the Yakima war, they declined the invitation. However, the goodwill of an entire tribe was soon destroyed through an insulting act by a few white men.

In February 1856, a government official of some unknown capacity had three Klickitat chiefs arrested, without just cause. The tribe became so angry at this injustice that they banded together with the Yakima tribe to inflict harm on their white neighbors with the aim of exterminating the lot or at the very least, driving them out of the West.

Erastus Joslyn, the first settler in the White Salmon–Bingen area, strongly opposed arresting the chiefs. Fearing exactly the type of retaliation that followed, he and his wife left for Portland under cover of darkness, leaving their claim entrusted to two men. Receiving advance notice of the impending attack early the next morning from a small group of friendly Klickitats, the property caretakers had barely made it across to Hood River when they saw the Joslyn home go up in flames. The Nathaniel Coe and William Jenkins families were the only residents of Hood River at the time, and they too watched the fireball ignite on the north shore. It was said that White Salmon Dave, a Yakima chief, was the one who set the home on fire.

The Indians mysteriously disappeared soon after burning the Joslyn property, leaving the Hood River crowd to wonder if this was the end of the conflict. Even the friendly Klickitats, who had joined the whites in Hood River, were confused by the disappearance. Settlers did the only logical thing: they tried to conduct business as usual. Farm work resumed at the Coe and Jenkins properties, with a few extra hands on deck. Rules were established among the families to allow them as much warning as possible, and provisions were made for sounding an alarm if the natives should return.

Unfortunately, they did return a few weeks later, making a clean sweep from the Yakima Valley through nearly every settlement in the southeastern part of the territory. This time, the 17 people in Hood River were alerted by a Klickitat couple, just in the nick of time. The parties made a quick decision to commandeer a nearby Indian canoe that was large enough to hold them all, then paddle upstream to The Dalles for safety at the fort. The few peaceful Klicktats who had ultimately refused to participate in the war were left in charge of the settlers' homes and asked to summon help if military forces should be spotted.

Joseph Hurst, the son born to James and Malinda Hurst shortly after their 1851 arrival in Oregon. Photo dated about 1875. Note the buckskin jacket and, no doubt, his "best" hat. Provided by Hurst family photo archives.

Shortly before reaching The Dalles, the settlers met up with the cavalry, which was going downriver by steamer. A skirmish ensued between the cavalry and the Indians. After leaving the Hood River–White Salmon area, most of the hostile Indians proceeded up the Cascades toward Puget Sound, to rendezvous with those who had crossed the northern Cascades in their war efforts. The white settlers returned to Hood River in a relatively short time, but it was several months before any of the local residents felt somewhat secure again.

A bloody battle broke out almost simultaneously with the Rogue River Indians in southern Oregon. Army regulars were sent south from their headquarters in Vancouver, Washington, and volunteers (attached as regulars) made their way through each community on the way down.

A call for volunteers was made by the governors of both the Washington and Oregon territorial governments. By a proclamation of the Oregon governor, Company B of the Oregon Mounted Volunteers was organized on October 11, 1855, under the command of Captain Orlando Humason, who later was known as the father of Wasco County. The Dalles Company B was dispersed to join the fight on November 24, 1855. Other leadership included General Joel Palmer and Colonel James W. Nesmith. Nathan Olney of The Dalles acted as Indian agent and Colonel George W. Wright of Fort Dalles commanded one major expedition. The majority of the troops were sent to fight the Yakima war and the balance to

Jonathan Keeney, Captain of Company C, Second Regiment, in the Rogue River War. Many of the men in Keeney's company moved to the Gorge when settlement was opened to the pioneers after the Indian wars.

fight at Rogue River. Some men began in the south and finished in the north, or vice versa.

Colonel Wright's tactics were controversial. His goal was to kill all Indian horses, leaving them on foot and helpless in the middle of winter. Another tactic found throughout the Indian wars was starving tribes into submission by keeping them from fishing, hunting, or raising crops or livestock. The Rogue River tribesmen who chose to fight, led by Tecumtum, took shelter in the Coast Range. Those who did not wish to fight, as well as women and children, sought shelter under the protection of regular Army troops at Fort Lane. They were escorted mid-winter to the Grande Ronde Reservation on the Oregon coast.

Some of the first pioneers to arrive at the scene of the battle from outside regions were Linn and Lane County men who moved their families east of the Cascades a few years after the war. Many of them were part of Company C of the Second Regiment under the command of Jonathan Keeney. Captain Keeney, it seems, had a clever way of looking at things and had a genuine fondness for his fighting men. The following story was told in the biography of one of his former soldiers in an 1889 history book:

> A freak storm which caused much merriment and some little trouble
> occurred in the Rogue River Mountains, amid the winter rain and mud,

when their horses—their own animals—were shivering in the damp, and growing to resemble greyhounds in figure. The order was given to take the horses to grass and recruit them up for the campaign in spring. Captain Keeney observed that he knew of some good grass in Linn county, and ordered his company home. This was not construed as desertion; and the Linn county boys proved their full fidelity some months later.

Thanks to information provided by Jonathan Keeney's great-grandnephew, Ralph Keeney of The Dalles, we can see how history is sometimes reformulated in order to soften the facts. The diary of Henry Robbins of Company C states that when Captain Keeney asked for a furlough on behalf of his men, he was told to "go to grass" by his superior officer. Keeney took it literally, not in error but quite intentionally, choosing to go to the best grass he knew of, back home near Brownsville. The colonel most likely meant something different, but it is one of those matters of history open to interpretation.

In June 1856, terms of the 1853 treaty were carried out with transfer of the tribe to reservations along the Oregon coast and reassertion of native fishing rights. The Army ordered a total ban on settlement east of the Cascades due to the unrest between the pioneers and Native Americans.

What is written about the Rogue River war in most historical accounts is something like this: "Fighting broke out in the Rogue River Valley in 1855 . . ." It is written that way because there is great disparity among first-person accounts of what triggered the war.

One variant has the Native Americans committing repeated predations on white settlers over a period of years, culminating in the brutal murders of more than a dozen people in 1855. Those events purportedly resulted in a group of pioneers waging a major counter attack. In another version, discussion among the higher powers of white society (exactly who was present for those discussions varies as well) reasoned that if a war started with the Indians, it would result in "employment" of many soldiers who would otherwise have no way to make a living. A recent drought had put a terrible strain on the local economy. Joseph Lane was openly in favor of wars and indicated to pioneers that war claims would be promptly and fairly settled by the government. Thus, a group of settlers are said to have intentionally triggered the wars with local tribes because it would result in an influx of cash into the economically distraught community. In the case of the simultaneous Yakima war, the murder of Indian Agent A.J. Bolin was allegedly a good excuse for the white community to stir up new trouble with the natives for the same purpose.

We will probably never know exactly how it all came about, but there is every indication in the words of the pioneers themselves that this cluster of Indian wars from 1853–1856 was at least encouraged by white men. Whether or not "serious predations" were first inflicted by pioneers or by Indian tribes is uncertain at best, since even minor squabbles between the two were unfailingly reported by the media as "Indian attacks" with editorial commentary included in the article.

Likewise, where pioneers were known to have committed acts upon the Native American population, the newspaper still called it an Indian attack and inevitably found some blame on the part of the Indians.

Although the rest of his comments were sometimes insulting to the native population, J. Ross Browne probably summarized the situation best in a letter to the Bureau of Indian Affairs on December 4, 1857. He said:

> The origin of the war is not different from that of any other Indian War. It is the natural result of immigration and settlement. . . . It was a war of destiny—bound to take place wherever the causes reached their culminating point . . . the history of our Indian Wars will show that the primary cause is the progress of [white] civilization, to which the inferior races, from their habits and instincts are naturally opposed. From the time of the landing of the Pilgrims on Plymouth Rock, to the present day we have had wars with the Indians, and they have all had a beginning. . . . But they either misunderstood the terms of the treaty [referring to the tribes' dissatisfaction with the 1853 treaty], or the

Just a portion of the day's fish bounty.
Library of Congress photo.

inducements held out to them to stop the war were such as it was not afterwards practicable to fulfill.

Aside from his air of superiority, he seemed to have a reasonably balanced view of the situation. What the Native Americans were clearly dissatisfied with was the loss of their traditional fishing rights. Feeding one's family is a basic need, not a misunderstanding.

On the other hand, John Beeson wrote a powerful letter to the editor of the *New York Tribune* on September 30, 1856, after his return from the Oregon Territory:

> I belong to the small minority in Oregon who believe with Generals [John Ellis] Wool and [Joel] Palmer, that the late war was unnecessary and cruel in the extreme, and that all the burning of property, the destruction of life and expenditure of public treasure, would have been saved if the civil authorities had administered equal justice instead of calling the people to arms. I have lived since the Fall of 1853 in Rogue River Valley, Southern Oregon, situated between the head waters of the Sacramento and the Willamette Valleys, and have had an opportunity of knowing much of the Indian tribes, both on the plains as well as the Pacific Coast.
>
> Notwithstanding the heartrending statements of savage barbarity which the Oregon papers have constantly spread before the public, it is a fact there are far more murdered Indians than Indian murderers; and when the whole truth is known, I believe it will appear that Indians are less savage than some who assume to be civilized. . . . To have submitted to robbery and outrage of the gravest kind without resentment would be more than Christian; to have remained passive and indifferent would be less than Men. I do not see under the circumstances how they could have done different or better than they have done, for practically they have only exclaimed with our own noble sires, "Give us liberty or give us death." And for this they have been denounced as not only savages, but as "varments" and demons unfit to live, and the military force of two Territories has been drawn out to destroy them from the earth.

He further states that certain public leaders and individuals were so outraged at his views, he had "fled in the darkness of night to Fort Lane, and was, by an escort of United States troops, conveyed beyond the scene of excitement."

The 1856 treaties, like so many others made with those earliest inhabitants, stripped the Native Americans of all but their most basic rights. Each tribe was situated on a sovereign reservation, given a small subsistence in the form of clothing and other necessities, plus restoration of their full fishing rights. What happened later to their reservation and rights is quite different than what was in the treaty.

Regardless of either war's true origins, pioneer soldiers risked life and limb to serve their country and many never returned from battle. Time and time again these same men had been asked to leave hearth and home—often when their homes were not yet finished—and provide manpower for the Indian wars. They had no inside knowledge of this conflict's beginnings, but simply did their duty. The same can be said for their opponents. These were the last major Indian wars in either the Yakima or Rogue River regions. Both tribes signed treaties in 1856.

On a lighter note about the 1850s, *Godey's Lady's Book*, a monthly magazine published in Philadelphia and distributed to all but the western territories, was a "proper" lady's ultimate reference in the nineteenth century. Even the women of lesser means read it whenever possible and attempted to assimilate as much of this information as possible into their daily lives. This, of course, was not a frequent option in the West. When a pioneer woman received a copy by mail or one managed to make it all the way across the plains with a new family, it was a guarantee of personal popularity. All the nearby ladies would congregate at their first opportunity to be schooled in the latest fashions and trends.

For the November 1850 issue topics included fashion, a literary discussion, a French language lesson, etiquette discussions, several poems, and a couple of short stories highlighting morals and principles of both men and women. The magazine's publishers were openly proud of the high-quality engravings used in each issue. The magazine gives us an idea what ladies on the western frontier were giving up. Imagine the wistfulness of a pioneer woman when she saw the engravings and read the following excerpted descriptions of the current fashions:

> To commence with out-door dress, it will be noticed that the favorite materials for walking costumes are merino, cashmeres, and silks. The first are exquisitely fine and soft, falling to the figure almost like mousseline.
>
> Figured [known as "prints" in today's language] cashmeres and mousselines are by no means in so good taste as the plain. There is always a wall-paperish effect. . . . The principal patterns are the palm leaf, bouquet, and wreath; a few are spotted, but no checks are worn by ladies, being entirely given up to the nether integuments of the sterner sex, where they flourish in all their breadth and depth of coloring.
>
> And now for shawls, cloaks, and mantillas, of which there is an endless host to choose from. Cashmere and India shawls will, of course, always be worn by those who can afford the enormous prices; though their imitations are so excellent as scarcely to be detected. For ourselves, we prefer the Parisian shawls. . . . But, then, they have not the prestige of the real India. Blanket, or tartan shawls are quite as much in favor as ever. A woolen shawl of this description is indispensible to the toilet of every lady; for morning promenades, evening wraps, or traveling, they are full of comfort.
>
> There is little change in the shape and style of bonnets—less than in almost everything else. The brims are more flowing, longer at the ears, and the crowns are flat once more, though slightly rounding on the edge.

The engravings used as magazine page illustrations were available for purchase as metal plate engravings, and it appears they did brisk business in sales of those

Walking-dress (left) and carriage-dress, which could also be used as a dinner-dress, each shown with the mantilla (cape) deemed appropriate by the fashion experts of Godey's Book. The dresses are made of silk and capes are of velvet, the cape on the right embellished with ermine trim.

plates, as was the custom of the day. Those of us who have heard the expression "She's no fashion plate" might now realize that the expression originated from this nineteenth-century practice of creating "fashion plates" for ladies' magazines.

One of the poems in the November 1850 issue presents a poignant look at one of the sad realities of a woman's life in that era:

THE SICK CHILD
By L.J.W.

THE twilight stars are dark to-night,
    The heavens are clouded o'er;
The moon will not come out as bright
    As she has done before.
The wind is weeping mournfully,
    I hear it even now—
I feel its fingers softly touch
    My hot and fevered brow.

I list the sighing of the breeze,
    And almost catch the tone
That whispers with the forest leaves,
    And echoes to their moan.
The streamlet dances playfully,

First Wasco County courthouse, built in 1859, is still in use today. Photo courtesy of Oregon State Archives.

In its unfettered flow,
And never did its gushing seem
    So musical and low.

But oh, my heart is sad to-night!
    What means this wild unrest?
My mother, come and lay my head
    More closely on thy breast;
And place thy soft, familiar hand
    Upon my burning brow—
Twill calm the wildness of my brain,
    That beats so madly now!

But hark, my mother, what bright forms
    Are those that float around,
With snowy robes and golden wings,
    And starry brightness crowned?
With softened eyes and sunny smiles,
    And looks of heavenly love,

They call me all their angel child,
    And beckon me above!

And Willie dear, who went to sleep,
    And never waked again,
Is with me now with a sunny brow,
    And he harps an angel strain;
And he calls to me with a silvery tone,
    And a look of melting love,
To come and take my golden harp,
    In the beautiful land above.

Oh, kiss me, mother, and let me feel
    Thy soft hand on my hair,
And I will go with the angel band,
    And pray for thy coming there!

As difficult as this frontier life was for everyone, it was a rapidly changing environment. Within the first five years of its existence, Wasco County's size was greatly reduced. The largest swath of land was lopped off in 1859 when Oregon was admitted as a state, limiting the county's reach to the far eastern edge of the current state boundaries. Everything east of the new border became part of the Washington Territory until it was again portioned out as the state of Idaho and small slices of Montana and Wyoming.

The difficulty of administering a district so large was not immediately evident, due to the fact that little county-wide business was conducted. It was fully realized, though, when Constable Dan Butler was called upon to serve a subpoena to a party near Fort Hall in what is now western Idaho. It took him more than six months to make the 1,000-mile round trip.

Over the next 50 years, 17 additional Oregon counties were formed east of the Cascades. Thus, many historical events that were recorded at the time as happening in Wasco County occurred in one of those other 17 counties. Those affected along the Gorge until the 1880s or later were Morrow, Gilliam, Sherman, and Hood River counties.

In 1857, the residents of The Dalles sent Colonel N.H. Gates to the legislature to introduce a bill for the incorporation of a city to be known as Dalles City, and it was passed and signed by Governor Curry. The city charter was written by Colonel Gates and granted on June 26, 1857. This was a signal of sorts that helped settlers to start making their way back over the mountains from the Willamette Valley.

Officers elected to serve under the first charter were N.H. Gates, president of the board; E.G. Cowne, R. Hall, B.F. McCormick, and P. Craig as trustees; C.R. Meigs, recorder; and Orlando Humason, who became treasurer. A new charter written by Humason was granted in 1859, which included a provision to elect regular city officials in place of trustees, and it also extended city limits to the second bluff. This was the first of several changes that have been granted to date. Colonel James K. Kelly became the first mayor of what is officially known as Dalles City, but today is generally referred to as The Dalles.

In 1858, the main places of business and their corresponding proprietors in The Dalles included A.H. Curtis's Wasco Hotel; W.D. Bigelow's grocery store; Bradford and Company's steamboat office; B.F. McCormick's Mount Hood Saloon; Powell and Company's saddle and harness shop; Trevitt and Cowne's saloon; James McAuliffe's grocery store; W.C. Moody's assay office; P. Craig's drug store; H.T. Isaacs's general merchandise store; R.R. Thompson and Company's warehouse; J. Juker's cigar store; W.L. DeMoss's bakery; The Umatilla House, operated by A.J. Nixon; and The Cushing Hotel, a boarding house and restaurant operated by N.H. Gates.

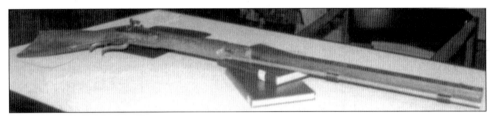

Captain Jonathan Keeney's rifle, now in possession of the Oregon Historical Museum. It was custom made from a Kentucky Long Rifle by Jonathan's father, John, between about 1830 and 1845, although the percussion lock was replaced in about 1850. Photo contributed by Ralph Keeney.

5. THE DEVELOPMENT YEARS

As territory became state on the south side of the Columbia River, things were also beginning to perk on the north side. The first settlers had found their way to White Salmon in 1852 in the form of Mr. and Mrs. Erastus S. Joslyn. The Joslyns came from Massachusetts to White Salmon via the Isthmus of Panama, traveling most of the distance by ship.

From all accounts, theirs was a quiet life, save for occasional encounters with unfriendly Native Americans, since no other white settlers appeared within visiting distance until 1862 when the Warners settled nearby. This small group started the lonely little White Salmon post office, which was run by Mr. Warner, later in the decade. It was located on his property, then known as Warner's Landing, but now is recognized as part of Bingen, Washington. According to an October 18, 1912 article in *The Enterprise* of White Salmon, both the Warners and Joslyns were friendly and accommodating to all who knew or would come to know them in the coming years. Even the Indians described them as "skookum man and woman." Had it not been for the unfortunate arrest of three innocent Klickitat chiefs (mentioned in the previous chapter), it would have been a perfect union.

Even in the 1860s, Barlow Road was no pleasure to navigate, although it was a little less treacherous in some places. Many westbound travelers were settling in the most established parts of eastern Oregon and southeast Washington Territory, nearest the Cascades. One of the trail emigrants in the Daily train of 1864, Miss Vanderburgh, painted a vivid picture of the process involved in going across a ridge just east of the Cascades and proceeding down the trail, followed by the trip over Barlow Road and down Laurel Hill on the west side:

> Later we found ourselves winding along the Deschutes Road, a trail hewn from solid rock and so narrow that in places there were but four inches outside the wheel track. Father was nearly frantic. Carrie with her three-horse team was ahead, and in no way could he pass the wagon to drive for her. A three-horse team, hitched as these were with two wheel horses and one leader, is a very hard team to handle. The cliff was so steep that he could not climb past her on the upper side and there was no room on the outside over the precipice beneath which the river

rushed. . . . There was nothing to do but watch her as she drove ahead, hugging the bank. The horses, however, were no more anxious than she to take that dreadful plunge. Far below, so far that they looked like toy people, I remember seeing a band of Indians [the Tygh tribe] catching some salmon and drying them about little smoky fires.

Finally reaching the end of Barlow Road, they paid the gatekeeper. Soon after the family encountered resistance from something other than geography:

Here for the first time on the journey, our right of way was challenged. As we drove through the gate an old billy goat disputed our right to pass. He looked so absurd, dancing about, his head nodding up and down as he threatened the big horses, that we all had to laugh. Evidently he did not like our appearance. Finally, rather than be driven over, he edged to the side of the road and we left him and his little band of goats behind, and headed for Barlow Pass.

About our camp many of the trees had been felled. The stumps were a puzzling sight to me. Fully twenty feet above the ground they had been chopped off with axes. I asked Father how it could have been done. He said they must have been cut in the winter when the snow lay on the ground. "Probably it was done by miners or prospectors," he said. "Wagons could not get through the pass when the snow was deep."

In the early 1860s, immigrants were settling in on the east side of the Oregon Cascades at the rate of dozens of families per year. Some settled in the recently incorporated Dalles City, near the old fort. Others began to populate the valleys and ridges south of the city and along the Deschutes River. The first outlying areas to be settled were, understandably, those nearest the rivers. A few adventurous souls took up claims just east of the Deschutes River in what would become the part of Sherman County known as Grass Valley. They would be isolated from most other pioneers east of the Cascades for a considerable period of time, due to the great distances between passable crossings on the Deschutes. The land they would farm was bordered by the most arid, desolate lands in the region. Still others—mostly single men and men who temporarily left their families west of the Cascades—made their way to mines in far eastern Oregon in hopes of making their fortunes.

Aside from the early missions, the first church on record east of the Cascades was Congregational Church, established in The Dalles on September 17, 1859, by Reverend W.A. Tenny. Charter members were Reverend and Mrs. W.A. Penfield, William Stilwell, Mr. and Mrs. Z. Donnell, and Mr. and Mrs. Thomas Joslyn. The relationship between Thomas Joslyn of The Dalles church and Erastus of White Salmon could not be determined by the author.

The church's original meeting place was in the courthouse. Members opted to move to other quarters before long, largely due to the constant disruptions occurring during their services. The jail was in the same building and prisoners

Walter Warner, most likely a son of the early Warners who settled on the Oregon side.

had their own ideas about the local environment. Services were frequently interrupted by inmates who took a shine to conducting their own "sermons" so loudly that the pastor's voice could not be heard. Likewise, prisoners preferred to sing different songs than the standard hymns and would often break out in full voice at inappropriate times.

The 1862 church rolls show the following regular members: Reverend Thomas Joslyn, W.D. Stilwell, E.S. Penfield, Zelek and Camilla Donnell, Robert Pentland, Governor Zenas Moody, H.J. Waldron, E.B. Comfort, Orlando Humason, John P. Booth, James B. Condon, Joshua French, Samuel Brooks, E.B. McFarland, Fred McDonald, R.A. Roscoe, W.R. Butcher, O. Sylvester, B.S. Huntington, and Mrs. E.R. Robinson.

A great innovation was added in the area on April 20, 1863. The recently-formed Oregon Steam Navigation Company completed a short but very significant section of railway that would greatly enhance shipping possibilities between the upper and lower Columbia River sections. Prior to this time, small water craft were used on the river above the rapids and steamers ran the lower part, but goods had to be hauled from one section of river to the other via a short portage road around the rapids. The new railway made it possible to haul large quantities of goods around the rapids, which encouraged settlement above the rapids and export of grain products from eastern Oregon to the worldwide market. The "Oregon Pony" was the first steam locomotive built on the Pacific coast and also holds the honor of being the first train operated in Oregon Territory. It can be seen on display at the Cascade Locks Museum today.

Faint traces of a controversial old wagon road can still be found in southeastern sections of Wasco County, a short distance from the tiny town of Antelope. It crosses and includes parts of the original pioneer and Indian trails between there and Canyon City. The road was known as The Dalles Military Road.

Early Americans, especially early pioneers to the western states, closely monitored government spending for waste or abuse. This particular project was heavily criticized by locals who had occasion to use the road after its completion. Unlike the many early controversies that quickly blew over, this one simmered for many years among the pioneers.

Congress approved the project on February 25, 1867. Road promoters obtained a grant of 592,557.8 acres on alternate sections of land between The Dalles and Fort Boise in what is now Idaho. The road was to extend "from The Dalles City, on the Columbia River, to Fort Boise, on the Snake River: Distance 330 1/2 miles." Total expenditures to build it were stated as $38,937.09—a princely sum in the 1860s. The Oregon Legislature approved the grant in October, 1868.

The route taken by the military road would be from The Dalles to Gordon's Bridge near the mouth of the Deschutes River, then upland to Mud Springs (later known as Erskine). From there it meandered to Haystack (later called Flanagan) and on to Cross Hollows (now Shaniko), which had an established stage station and was soon to become a key location for worldwide commerce. The route continued through Maupin stage station, which was shown as "Moppin" on military maps of the day. It should be noted that the stage station was located just a couple of miles east of what later became the town of Antelope. The station, as

Some of the smaller ferries used between Hood River and White Salmon in later years, these little boats were real workhorses in the early days. Even after steamers arrived on the upper Columbia, a majority of shore-to-shore business was done via flatboat. Courtesy of Hood River County Historical Museum.

well as the town, was named for station operator Howard Maupin, who was much celebrated in the pioneer community for killing the unruly Chief Paulina in an 1867 bloodbath. The town of Maupin came to existence several miles northwest of the stage station, which causes a great deal of confusion for many family historians who try to learn more about ancestors who settled nearby or traveled through the Maupin stage stop en route to another location.

Still following the pioneer trail fairly closely, the military road went southeast from the Maupin stage stop to the gold mining town of Canyon City, and continued east to Fort Boise in what is now Idaho. Acceptance of the road by Oregon Governor George L. Woods of The Dalles was contingent upon his personal inspection of the entire road. He took W.M. Hand of *The Dalles Mountaineer* newspaper along for the ride, where Hand wrote an extensive report published thereafter. The road was approved by Governor Woods on June 23, 1869.

So what caused the controversy over this road? The first objections came because it was built after the gold rush in eastern Oregon had subsided. This discovery was so short-lived that it might have been difficult for anyone to realize a road was needed until it was too late, yet that was immaterial to those who objected. What really bothered people was spending so much money for the meager quality of the end product.

A major road in that era would have been built by clearing the land of vegetation using a combination of men, horses, and oxen to push and pull on a variety of boards and other equipment to grade the road bed flat. Once it was ready, rough wooden planks would be used as a surface, much as we use pavement now. Even the little portage road around the Columbia River rapids constructed more than 25 years earlier had been built in this fashion. Although the price tag would give one the illusion that The Dalles Military Road would be built to accommodate a large volume of travelers, reality was quite a different story.

It was a bumpy, dusty (or muddy) mess a good share of the time, and no planks or timbers were used. Harvey W. Scott, editor of *The Oregonian*, may have said it best in his article dated June 26, 1869: "A large part of this 'road' was built simply by driving an ox-cart over the country while two men trudged behind with shovels on their shoulders." This statement was most likely a bit of an exaggeration, but it wasn't a smooth road. Without any form of true automation, it's hard to imagine building a road through 330 miles of alternating mountains and desert in a single lifetime, much less making all 330 miles smooth. Don't you wish we knew why the local settlers were expecting a freeway in the dust?

It is unknown by anyone still living whether or not a certain branch road was an impromptu addition to the road when it was built, or if it was merely a case of poor judgement and high hopes by an adjacent land owner who added it shortly thereafter. The one in question comes off the main road at the confluence of the Deschutes and John Day rivers a short distance southeast of where Antelope now stands. Its builder seems to have constructed it in the worst possible location: down a steep embankment to Fir Creek, then over Curran and Muddy creeks. This branch saw so little use that no trace of it could be found just 20 years later.

People often traveled by stage in those days when they needed to cover great distances, but speed was not a factor. Regardless of weather and road conditions, stage fares between The Dalles and Canyon City ranged between $25 and $40 per traveler, depending on the decade in which travel took place and the stage company used. This is a cost of somewhere in the neighborhood of 9 to 12 days' pay to experience 197 miles of thrills that might include sliding off an icy road, getting stuck in a foot or two of mud or snow, choking on desert dust, bumping over sagebrush, dodging huge tumbleweeds, and other interesting possibilities.

Nonetheless, things were coming together east of the Cascades. As communities formed, the wheels of progress were set in motion and people were poised for success to follow their hard work. They wouldn't have to wait much longer to start realizing their dreams. They were learning to work the quirks to their advantage; using carefully-honed skills they either brought with them or acquired on arrival, fine-tuning them along the way. As you will see, ranchers and stockmen held a great deal of admiration for one another's skills.

Of the few memoirs to be found about that period in the history of the Gorge and its communities, these written by Albert Jay Price most clearly describe skills important to the stockmen in those early years. The Price-Masiker family's experiences, both on the plains and in the West, appear to be typical of most families who came to Oregon country. This is how Jay described the stockmen of the early days:

> In about 1875 or 76 the Walker boys took up a ranch near Gordon Butte. They had sheep and some horses. There were six boys. Morgan and Elmer were deaf mutes. Joe Walker and young Tom Gordon had a shooting scrape over a fence. Joe lost an arm and Tom was killed. Joe was tried for murder, but was finally acquitted. George Reeder had a horse ranch near the Walker place. He came there soon after the Walkers did. Two or three years later Dave Daugherty was with Reeder. They each had some horses and they gathered up all the stray horses they could find and left the country between two days. I think Reeder sold his place to old man Bash. Dave stole Ida Bash. They were married at Walla Walla. They went to Montana. Bill Walker went with the outfit. He was the only one of the lot that ever came back.
>
> Frank Fulton was a splendid judge of range cattle. When eastern buyers bought cattle in those early days, they paid different prices for cows and calves, and dry cows, yearlings, two and three year-olds. The buyers and the sellers usually chose Frank to judge the age, and kind as they passed through the chute and seldom was his judgement questioned.
>
> Once a "critter" was going through the chute that belonged to Henry Barnum. Frank called it a two-year-old steer, although he knew it was a long yearling. The buyers were satisfied, but Barnum claimed it was a three-year old. Frank told him he had better let it go as a two, but he would not. So it was examined and passed as a yearling. Barnum, who

could have had the price of a two, wanted the price of a three, and had to take the price of a yearling, and the joke was on him.

It is my belief that C.I. Helm was the best judge of horses in this county. After he had taken his horses to the Big Bend country, he went east and made a study of draft horses in several of the largest cities, and decided that the Percherons were the best horses for the eastern market. He bought some Percheron stallions, which he shipped west, and raised some splendid horses.

I believe that Jim Pearson was the best roper that ever grew up in this country. A rope was his plaything from the time he could walk. The next year after he went to the Big Bend he made 97 throws without a miss, catching both hind feet. This was not done as an exhibition, nor was it done all in one day, but was done as range work day after day. A cattleman offered to bet 100 head of cattle that Jim was the best roper in the state of Washington at that time. The bet was never taken.

There were many other good ropers in this country. John Brookhouse, Ed Gibson, Ed Floyd and Bill Pearson were among the best. Frank Fulton carried the longest rope and swung the biggest loop of any man on the range.

Price's memoir goes on to name the men he believed to be the best riders of the area during the 1860s and 1870s. It is evident from his emphasis on those skills, as well as from other commentary found in newspapers prior to about 1920, that

James and Malinda Hurst and two of their sons, sometime prior to 1908. Provided by Hurst family photo archives.

Gorge society was a shining example of what is now viewed as the quintessential "cowboy culture" of the early West.

When pioneers settled east of the Cascades in the 1850 and 1860s, they had left behind a comparatively cushy life. Even moving from the west to the east side of the Cascades was a considerable step backward in terms of ease, as a great deal of development had already taken place in the Willamette Valley. Many of those who came directly from midwestern states brought family elders with them who had already opened up a new frontier some 40 to 60 years earlier. Every generation seemed determined to set out for the most primitive living conditions they could find.

Many of those who came over from the Willamette Valley did so to get away from the "crowd" forming there: by 1860, Oregon's total population had ballooned to 52,465 residents, compared to just over 11,000 a decade earlier, with the vast majority living west of the Cascades. Others came to the east side to enjoy the drier climate either for health or aesthetic reasons.

A pleasant summer afternoon in one of the Hood River Valley's orchards, Mount Hood in the background. Oregon State Highway Commission photo, courtesy of Hood River Company Historical Museum.

As exciting as those times were for the farmers and ranchers, work wasn't the only thing happening east of the Cascades. Exploration of the less readily-accessible areas was taking place then as it still is today. Give a man a mountain and he has to climb it to see what he can find. Many mountains along the Gorge offer great views, but the one that has attracted the greatest amount of attention and offers the most spectacular views is Mount Hood. The following article appeared in the July 23, 1869 issue of *The Mountaineer*:

A party composed of Mr. J.J. Springer, of Lancaster, Pa., correspondent for the Lancaster Intelligencer, and Messrs. Geo. Liebe, James Pursee, Geo. Munger, with Silky Smith and an Indian as guides, left The Dalles on Friday afternoon last for a trip to Mount Hood. The party took a southerly direction on an old Indian trail, crossing Three Mile Creek about eight miles from town, then crossed over to Eight Mile Creek, where they made their first camp some three miles above Doyle's farm.

The next day they camped at a beautiful cold spring near the head of Fifteen Mile Creek [near what is now Dufur]. While here the party ascended to the top of a huge rock from which they obtained a magnificent view of Mount Hood and the surrounding country. The following day the party descended to a beautiful lake, the headwaters of the Tygh; then descended the mountain and crossed White River, and passed up White River to the foot of Mount Hood, where they made their third camp. That evening they viewed out a route to ascend Mount Hood.

Next morning about half-past three the party started for the summit. The entire party, except the Indian guide, who could not be hired to accompany them, owing to the fact, as he said, "that there was a big tyee [Indian of another tribe] up there who would kill him with stones if he did so," got about two-thirds of the way up when they weakened all except Geo. Liebe and Silky Smith, who continued on to within about five hundred feet of the top, when Smith concluded he had enough of it and would not go any further.

Mr. Liebe continued on to within one hundred feet of the top, when he came to a perpendicular ledge of rocks and ice, with a deep chasm so situated, that if he missed his footing he would have fallen to a great depth, and as he was all alone he did not feel justified in making the attempt. Mr. Liebe says that the smell of sulfur was very strong [on the way up the mountain] and made several of the party feel sick at the stomach.

The party returned by way of Barlow's Gate on the old Emigrant road, intersecting the road about seven miles from the foot of Mount Hood and about twenty-two miles west of Barlow's Gate. Mr. Liebe says that the route by way of the Tygh [Valley] and the Emigrant road is by far the best and most practicable. It is his opinion that no woman ever ascended Mount Hood, and he thinks it very doubtful whether anybody has ever been to the top. Notwithstanding, he thinks he can make the ascent, and is willing to try it again.

Parties wishing to make the trial: Mr. Liebe believes September would be the best month to do so. A coat, several canes, and a number of fishing lines were found about five hundred feet below where Mr. Liebe was, no doubt left there by some party who wished to mark the spot where they had ascended to. The [Liebe] party returned on Wednesday, much pleased with their trip and without accident.

The Liebe climb followed the first officially documented attempt at climbing Mount Hood by almost exactly 12 years, so it was by no means one of the first attempts. It was, however, one of the earliest documented climbs to an altitude so near the 11,239-foot summit. In the absence of a breathing apparatus, the thin air was more than likely the reason so many of the party "weakened" and "felt sick at the stomach" by the time they were within a few thousand feet of the top.

As some were pushing their personal limits using the natural surroundings, others were attempting to establish the area as a viable economic workhorse. Have you ever seen a coin marked with "1876 T" or a similar date? It may have been the mark used for coinage created in The Dalles Mint, if it had ever actually produced a coin. Tucked away between blocks of downtown The Dalles stands a stone building containing a fun piece of history. A concrete addition that faces Second Street currently houses a telecommunications company, but the original fortress-style stone building at the center of the block is not actively used. In fact, it never was used for its original purpose.

Congress appropriated funding in 1864 to build a new federal mint there. It would strike coinage using metal from Canyon City and other mining operations in eastern Oregon, giving the Pacific Northwest its own mint. Unfortunately, Canyon City's yield slowed down considerably within a short time after the new mint building was underway. By the time it was finished nearly two years after the scheduled completion date, there was little gold to be found in any of the state's mines. The Oregon gold rush was literally a flash in the pan. One of the most ironic reasons for the construction delay was due to so many construction laborers leaving to work in the gold mines! Other factors that contributed to the difficulty of raising the building included cost over-runs, weather, and even flooding according to some sources.

The building was a fine two-story structure though, built with hand-hewn stone brought in by wagon from nearby Mill Creek. When the federal government abandoned the project in 1870, it deeded the property over to the state of Oregon for charitable or educational use. Of course the state would need to add a roof if the building were to ever be used as an enclosure, but it seemed to be a fairly minor detail at the time in view of what Oregon would gain. The state deeded the property to Wasco Independent Academy (a local school) at a later date, but it was never used for education. Later still, a large concrete block addition was added and has since been used by a variety of business interests.

The settling in and setting up that took place in the 1860s laid firm groundwork for the decades to follow. Pioneer families had established themselves in no uncertain terms throughout most of the Gorge communities and they were poised for success. As more poured into the area east of the Cascades in the 1870s, the early families began to see the fruits of their labors, both figuratively and literally. The grueling work and heartbreaks of the past decades began to pay off.

They were about to experience the boom phase of the 1870s and 1880s.

Downtown The Dalles near the turn of the century. A dentist's office, an unnamed bakery, and the New York Cash Store on the left. The Pioneer Bakery and Snipes & Kinnersley Druggists on the right, among others. Courtesy of The Dalles Chronicle.

6. Carving a Niche in World economics

By 1870, the local economy was beginning to resemble what was left behind by the pioneers when they left the Midwest. Ranches and orchards were planted and some were beginning to produce; business cores were forming in a few towns to form a downtown area. Some experimental fruit plantings had begun to produce in the Hood River Valley and across the river at White Salmon. Strawberries were the only plants mature enough to produce this quickly, but fruit trees were growing nicely and promising good yields for the future. Orchardists could already tell what some of the best crops would be in each of the Gorge's varied climates. Every local home had a garden and most were producing more than enough to keep associated families supplied with vegetables and fruit.

Wheat ranchers had spent several seasons learning how often they should rotate their crops in each field, the best times to plant for maximum yield of a single crop or the bounty of two harvests, and how to try to outfox Mother Nature so the entire crop wouldn't be ruined by an unexpected but thorough soaking right before harvest time. Ranchers and orchardists were learning the limits of this new soil.

Climate is one of the most unique aspects of the communities along the Columbia River Gorge, progressing from a self-watering forest at Multnomah Falls to hillsides and meadows at Hood River and White Salmon, to hearty grasslands in the valley around The Dalles. Increasingly arid land lies to the east and south, as well as east and north of Goldendale on the Washington side. Those early settlers were acutely aware of the almost startling changes in climate that could be felt within a mere 20-mile horse and buggy ride.

With the O.R. & N line running the rails near the portage road each day and regular steamer service established below the rapids, crops and livestock could easily be shipped out of the area. Local producers of all kinds would soon come to realize the true potential of this seemingly small benefit, for it would open them up to world commerce. The three ferries running above the rapids kept people reasonably mobile, too.

Although several ranchers had settled within 15 to 20 miles of The Dalles during the 1860s, only a handful of them ventured to start their operations in the semi-arid prairies of central Oregon. The Antelope Valley wasn't friendly looking from a rancher's standpoint due to a lack of accessible water. However, a few did make the mental connection between the abundant rye grasses and the resident animals for whom the valley was named. The few who made the association, and were willing to gamble on their futures to a degree, would be greatly rewarded in the coming years.

Some of the earliest impact of Gorge industry on the world market came in the form of sheep that were perfectly suited to the arid climate and grasses grown on the fringes of the desert. Their prong-horned cousins, the Antelope, had survived quite nicely in this environment for many years prior to the white man's arrival in the West. Willamette Valley ranchers had been grazing their cattle east of the Cascades during the past decade, making use of the resources that were far more abundant there than in their own area. A nearly perfect natural environment east of the Cascades awaited anyone with a desire to own a sheep ranch, and a few wise ranchers seized the opportunity. Their good management of resources would soon put Antelope Valley on the map worldwide.

During the 1870s and 1880s, local stage and freight service became the primary means of transporting goods overland. The stage routes all intersected

B.R. Tucker fruit packing plant in Hood River, early 1900s. Photo by W.D. Rogers, courtesy of Hood River County Historical Museum.

An early locomotive runs the rails around a bend in the Gorge. Courtesy of The Dalles Chronicle.

at Cross Hollows, which was later named Shaniko. Goods could be moved in any direction from there: southeast through Canyon City to the far reaches of eastern Oregon and into Idaho, south to Prineville and the Klamath Basin, or north to either Biggs or The Dalles for further shipment along the Columbia by steamer.

The Imperial Stock Ranch was founded in 1871 by Richard Roland Hinton near where the village of Bakeoven now stands, outside of Shaniko. He arrived from the Willamette Valley at the age of 19 with only his saddle horse, a pack horse, and his six-shooter when he built a sod house into a dugout in the earth and lived in it for several years while proving up on his homestead. He married Mary Emma Fitzpatrick in 1872, taking his new bride to the dugout soddy to live. Twelve years later, he received title to the first plot of land.

A son, James E. Hinton, was born to the couple in 1874, and the dugout soddy served as delivery room for the birth. Daughter Lillian was born two years later, but it appears that the family may have lived in a temporary above-ground home by then. Their final residence was not completed until 1900, but it was well worth waiting for. Mary worked alongside her husband as she tended their children, to create a good, working ranch. They started out with just a small herd of sheep and gradually added hay and wheat to the ranch's production as the number of animals grew. The hay would provide food and bedding for the ranch's wide variety of animals and the wheat was produced for profit to be poured back into the ranch as an investment.

Other sheep ranchers had already begun their operations on a small scale slightly north of where Hinton settled. Hinton was one of the first landowners in the Shaniko area. Over the long term, he certainly had the largest holdings, but his was not the only successful operation in the valley.

A few sheep ranchers began to import other breeds, introducing new bloodlines, and most importantly, breeding for better wool. Mr. Hinton came up with a new hybrid he called the Columbia sheep and continued to breed his stock for those same traits, building his herd into a wool empire over a 30-year period. Meanwhile, he developed a unique management plan allowing for maximum yield of native ryegrass and bunchgrasses without unnecessarily burdening those natural resources.

Sheep ranching operations throughout the region grew larger than life in the 1880s and 1890s due to a fabulous market and excellent natural resources. Cross Hollows gained the unofficial title of wool shipping capital of the Northwest. It has even been touted as the wool shipping capital of the world from the 1880s well into the 1900s, but this can't be confirmed as fact. However, to get the wool to market required using every form of transportation available in the time period.

Some of the wool was shipped out of Shaniko on special pack trains and large wagons, then taken for further travel by rail to a waiting steamer that would take it down the Columbia to be loaded onto another ship for international shipment. Some of it was taken via the Santiam Wagon Road (also known as the Willamette Valley and Cascade Mountain Military Road) for purchase by Willamette Valley woolen mills or an agent of Pendleton Woolen Mills.

Built primarily as a stock road and operated by a group of Willamette Valley businessmen, The Santiam Wagon Road toll records clearly show the impact of eastern Oregon sheep ranches on the Willamette Valley's economy. As early as the 1870s, approximately half of the total number of tolls in the gatekeeper's records—eventually well over half of the total dollar value—were in the form of live sheep going east or half-mile long trains of wagons filled with wool westbound to area woolen mills. The tolls for four-horse and six-horse teams were $3 and $3.50 respectively, while a pack horse was just 50¢, a cow 10¢, and a pig or sheep a mere 3¢. When the Columbia Southern Railroad line reached Shaniko in 1901, there was an immediate and dramatic decline in toll road revenues. From that point forward, all wool bound for the Willamette Valley left Shaniko by rail.

Stockmen throughout the Gorge communities were busy throughout the 1870s and into the 1880s, moving a massive amount of horses and cattle from one western range to another. Many rangelands were converted to wheat and oat fields during this time , as ranchers discovered just how well suited the soil was for grain production. Wheat was the clear winner and cattle were moved to less profitable soil to graze. Some herds were taken to various ranges in the Northwest, while others were driven as far east as Chicago.

The winter of 1881–1882 was so severe, it nearly wiped out the area's cattle ranchers. Thousands of head of cattle perished in the cold and snow, causing several ranchers to go broke. Those with great losses sold off their small remaining numbers, and many began wheat ranching from that point forward. Those who bought the remainder stock took their herds to other locations, but some smaller operations replenished their stock and stayed in the local area.

Wheat production was becoming a major part of the economy east of the Cascades. The population was increasing steadily, with the majority of the settlement created between 15 and 30 miles of the Columbia River. Although transportation was still fairly primitive, several small settlements had grown on both the Washington and Oregon sides of the river, extending the Gorge's population reach all the way east to present day Arlington (then called Alkali) in Oregon and Roosevelt in Washington.

A.H. Jewett arrived on the Washington side, staking a claim in 1874. The White Salmon school district was organized around 1876, with a fellow by the name of Levison as its first teacher in the new schoolhouse near Salmon Falls. A cabin on Jewett's land served as the schoolhouse sometime thereafter. The school district was divided in 1880 between Bingen and White Salmon, at which time the White Salmon district built a new school at a cost of $500.

Education was an interesting thing in those times, regardless of location. For those readers who have been frustrated by the difficulty of finding ancestors listed in a census or tax listing, it might be easier to understand why the problem occurs if we realize that spelling was not a big part of school curriculum until late in the nineteenth century. Even surnames weren't spelled consistently by their owners,

Mr. Covey and his best friend, a Springer Spaniel, take a buggy ride.

so spellings of other words were even less important to most people. The following memo is the actual transcribed statement of an 1865 census taker elsewhere in the country:

> I am a census taker for the city of baffalow. our city has groan very fast in resent years and now in 1865 it has becum a hard and time comsuing job to count all the peephill. There are not many that can do this work as it is nesesarie to have a good ejchashum, which a lot of pursons still do not have. Anuther atribeart need for this job is good spelling, for meny of the peephill to be counted can hardly speek inglish, let alone spel there names!

White Salmon Congregational Church was built in October 1879, with Reverend George H. Atkinson serving as pastor. Charter members included Mrs. J.R. Warner, Mrs. Cynthia E. Warner, Mrs. Arabella Jewett, A.J. Thompson, John Purser, Mrs. Mary Purser, George Swan, Mrs. Mary Anne Swan, and Mrs. Martha Purser. A succession of pastors tended the flock throughout the 1880s, including Reverend F.H. Balch, who later wrote "Bridge of the Gods." Some of the same pastors served Congregational churches simultaneously in Lyle, Washington, and in Hood River on the Oregon side, traveling back and forth by ferry or in canoes and small flatboats.

The Suksdorf family moved to the lower landing (Bingen) at White Salmon in the late 1870s. From almost the moment the Jewetts and Suksdorfs met, there was trouble between them. It is generally accepted that the location or name of the post office was at the root of the disagreements between the two parties, but it may have merely been a result of the Jewetts' reactions to the brusque nature of the immigrant German Suksdorfs.

Whatever the cause, there was an ongoing feud between those early settlers and it ultimately resulted in the Suksdorfs settling the village of Bingen down on the landing and the Jewetts digging their heels in up on the bluff, in the area that would retain the name of White Salmon. Determined to preserve a connection to their German heritage, the Suksdorfs named Bingen after a town of the same name on the Rhine River in Germany. The feud was so bitter and all-consuming that when the railroad arrived a number of years later, the station would be called the Bingen-White Salmon station.

The most prolific industries on the Washington shore prior to the 1890s were dairying and stock raising. The Jewetts established a plant stock nursery, thereby providing new settlers with stock that would eventually form the area's orchards. The White Salmon post office was moved from Warner's Landing, which had just become part of Bingen, up to White Salmon when Jacob Hunsaker established a store signaling the true beginning of White Salmon's retail section.

By this time the family dog was making a noticeable appearance in the West, similar to the way pioneers remembered having an old hound dog in the Midwest. Every animal had a job to do, which meant the family dogs were generally either sleeping or working when the children of the family wanted to play with them. As children will do, they improvised to suit their needs, adopting such interesting "pets" as crawdads, squirrels, chipmunks, and wild birds. The favorites were as varied as the children who adopted them, but rescuing injured animals was a universal pastime, as Charlotte Matheny Kirkwood illustrates in her story, "Pioneer Pets":

It was while we lived at this place that Fanny was given to me. One day Father found the carcass of a deer. It had been freshly killed and cougar tracks were all around everywhere. He came home for things that he needed and help to build and set a big trap. He baited it with what was left of the deer and waited for the cat to return to its kill. Father waited for a day and a night, then went back to the trap, sure enough, it had been sprung. Not by the panther, as he hoped and expected, but by a little brown-eyed, spotted fawn. She had come to what was left of her mother, and Father found her there in the big pit frightened, starved and chilled, so he wrapped her in his big blue army cape and carried her home to me.

She was the only fawn that I owned. Father caught her when she was two months old, or maybe less. Warm milk to drink and a corner at the side of the open fire to curl up in and Fanny was as happy as a petted kitten. Coyotes or wolves would have eaten her if we had left her outside at night, just as they would have eaten the big broken winged Sandhill crane, if he had been left outside. He did not care about the fire, but was quite contented to sleep under Isaiah's bed. Isaiah had run him down and caught him somewhere out on the prairie. He had fought as only a Sandhill crane can fight, trying with all his might to peck out Isaiah's eyes. Isaiah was scratched and bloody and the crane was too exhausted to more than flutter when Isaiah came home with him dangling over his shoulder.

He was a funny old thing. His long, ungainly awkward legs were out of all proportion to the rest of him. Sometimes he would get out into the floor and do the funniest clattery shuffle, nodding and bowing and scraping his big feet on the puncheons. He would keep it up till he was quite exhausted and until everyone who watched him was exhausted too. The harder we laughed, the faster he whirled and hopped in his stupid, ridiculous dance.

At night he would get down on his knees and creep under Isaiah's bed. The puncheons were rough and hard and his quarters were cramped and entirely unsuitable for a Sandhill crane. He was mighty uncomfortable. We could tell that because every time we happened to be awake 'nnch, nnch' we could hear his rusty old knees shuffling about on the bare boards.Isaiah thought a lot of his crane. By spring his broken wing had mended and was quite as good as ever. He was allowed to go and come as he willed. Sometimes he would stay away

The big snow of 1885 in downtown The Dalles. On right, Dr. Siddall's dentistry practice resides appropriately next door to the liquor store, followed by a cigar store, bakery, and Snipes & Kinnersly's drug store. At left, another drug store, W.R. Abrams tinsmith, and Wingate & Company There are men on the Wingate roof, attempting to relieve the burden of snow.

for several days. His coming became more and more uncertain, his temper too, became uncertain and we were not altogether sorry when he finally left us entirely to live and dance with those of his own kind.

The 1880s were filled with surprises. As we might expect, a few of them were unpleasant. The harsh winter of 1881–1882 may have been an omen of sorts for the decade to come.

The Dalles businesses and residents were given a warning on January 23, 1881 when a serious fire broke out downtown. Half a block's worth of buildings were completely consumed by the fast-moving fire, from the corner of Second and Washington streets extending to First Street buildings. Virtually no businesses or homes were covered by insurance in the nineteenth century, so pioneer families were forced to bear the losses and try to move on. This fire came just a decade before an even worse blaze tore through the downtown area (discussed in Chapter nine).

During the 1870s and 1880s, rails were being laid as fast as crews could be appropriated. The West was preparing for the day it would be linked by railroad with the East Coast. Telegraph lines had been operational since the late 1860s in all towns along the main and most future rail lines. The foundations for shortline railroads were being laid in every burg, running in every direction, with the idea of forming a network to eventually link even the most remote areas by rail with the cities. On December 18, 1884, the Pioneer Express locomotive left The Dalles carrying 148 passengers, bound for Portland during a blizzard. The train didn't get very far: it became sandwiched between two avalanches a short distance east of what is now Cascade Locks, with 25-foot snow drifts both behind and in front of it. A relief party finally reached the stranded train on foot a week later on Christmas Day, bringing with them a hog from Hood River. The hog served as both sustenance and holiday dinner for the passengers, who had been without food the entire time. The train was able to retreat to The Dalles on December 30 and, after the westernmost avalanche was cleared from the tracks, the Pioneer Express finally made it all the way to Portland a week later.

The arrival of the railroad was not entirely positive, for an easy connection to the rest of the United States brought with it easier access to deadly disease. One of the worst to make its way to the Gorge was diphtheria, which arrived with a vengeance shortly after the cross-country rail system was in place. Many local children lost their lives in the epidemic, as did a number of adults. By far, the saddest of those situations befell the Albert L. Savage family, when nearly everyone in the household was stricken with the disease. Albert was one of the early Wasco County deputy marshals and then was county commissioner. Only one child, Erastus, was spared from diphtheria. A mere child himself, he buried six younger siblings in six little graves at the Lone Pine Cemetery in Wamic on Nov 27, 1879. His parents were too sick and weak to even get out of bed to help bury them.

A short distance east of The Dalles lies the northwestern Sherman County line. Sherman County was created in 1889 out of the northeast corner of Wasco County. It was named for General William Tecumseh Sherman of Civil War fame. The county is bounded by the Columbia River on the north, the John Day River and Gilliam County on the east, and the Deschutes River, Buck Hollow, and Wasco County on the west and south. The tiny county's population has remained surprisingly constant since its beginnings, hovering just below a total of 2,000 residents. It is strictly an agricultural area, entirely devoid of industry. A large portion of its 831 square miles is under cultivation, more than any other county in Oregon, with the majority of cash crops in wheat and barley. Cattle ranches and river-based recreation also contribute to the economy.

It seems fitting to end this chapter about the 1880s with a few excerpts from Jay Price's memoirs about Sherman County ranchers, followed by a comment of second-generation pioneer Joe Gray in the final years of his life. Jay was born in the 1860s and Joe in the 1890s, yet their youthful exploits were virtually identical in many ways. This might lead us to believe that, even with the great advances

Henry Villard's Golden Spike Train stops in The Dalles for a celebration on the first cross-country journey by rail, which began in Portland (1883). Columbia Hotel in background. Photo courtesy of The Dalles Chronicle.

made between the 1860s and the early 1900s, life retained the flavor of the Old West for a very long time. In the words of Jay Price:

> I will name just a few of the first to settle there. About the first was Dr. Rollins in Grass Valley, Gil Woodworth, Henry Jory, Charley Barzee, Owen and Hugh Scott, Corson, Medler, McCoy, the Moores from California, Biggs, Murchie, McPherson, Sink, Belshee, and of course many others moved there before 1885.
>
> My parents sold the old place in 1883 and moved to Columbus, Washington, later to Yakima, Kennewick and Hood River, and in 1907 to Grants Pass. Mother passed on at the age of 85 and Dad almost 88.
>
> In conclusion, I will tell one on myself. When I was 12 years old I was a good rider. One day I was riding a wild cayuse, and he had given up the idea of throwing me, but was not bridle wise. We had drifted over in to Spanish Hollow, two miles below Eatons, when my horse saw some horses and decided to go to them, but there was a deep V-shaped ditch between. I tried to stop him, but he reared and bucked around and fell in the ditch and slid back down in the ditch, with me still in the saddle. He was on my left leg, and the more he kicked the more he crowded me. I could not get out, so I undone the cinch, in hopes that he could get up,

but he could not. Soon I heard a horse running and Nate Eaton rode up on the bank and soon pulled the cayuse off of me. He was on a high hill a mile away and saw us fall in the ditch. My leg was badly bruised, otherwise I was alright. I certainly always had a warm spot in my heart for Nate Eaton.

Being a cowboy-in-the-making was a matter of pride with the younger generation even after the turn of the century. Joseph Aden Gray (1890–1981), who grew up on a wheat and cattle ranch near Victor in the southern part of Wasco County, loved to tell about his early years in vivid detail well into his 90th year of life. One of his fondest memories was of honing his riding skills with his elder brother, John (1887–1962). He referred to their riding exploits as when they were "little buckaroos."

A native family takes temporary shelter along the river, late nineteenth century. The white in the background on the shore is thick smoke billowing around a white tent—most likely their fish smokehouse. Courtesy of Hood River County Historical Museum.

7. TRAGEDY AND TRIUMPH: TESTING THE PIONEER SPIRIT

The 1890s started out innocently enough in the Columbia Gorge. Things had never been better than they were right then. Without question, the entire area was bustling with business and fresh starts, the economy was at a peak, and the heavens seemed to be smiling upon every new thing attempted in the Gorge.

The Dalles Chronicle distributed its first issue on December 15, 1890. Little did the publisher realize just how much news there would be to report during the first few years of the newspaper's existence.

Stages operated smoothly on well-established routes; commerce was at an all-time high; wheat, wool, and fruit were being shipped out of the area in record volumes; telegraph lines had been operational for a few decades; railroads were operating efficiently, and a big electrification project was making its way through the Gorge.

Some of the best information about the Gorge's history is found in vintage newspapers. No amount of third-party writing could possibly convey what the following news clippings from *The Dalles Chronicle* tell us. The cheeky descriptions are worth reading even if the subject matter fails to interest the reader:

> Tuesday, January 6, 1891—Some wretch with no fear of the law, and no regard for the rights of others, last night helped himself to a set of single buggy harnesses belonging to Mr. Jud Fish. The thief emptied a sack filled with pitch kindling wood, and evidently used the sack to carry off the harness in. The same fellow probably stole two collars from a teamster at Books & Beers, and got away with a whip from someone else. From indications the fellow will have a horse before long, so it is well enough to lock the stable doors now.
>
> The west bound Fast Mail distinguished itself this morning by giving birth to a bouncing girl baby, or rather a woman on the Fast Mail did so. Conductor Coleman was in charge of the train and received an intimation of what was about to happen after the train left

Umatilla. A physician on the train was summoned, several kind ladies volunteered their services and the young lady was ushered into the world as the train rushed along the bank of the Columbia at the rate of twenty-five miles an hour. We suggest that according to the eternal fitness of things she should be named Columbia. Thus again is the wonderful productiveness of Oregon exemplified, and the climate given another boom.

Misfortunes never come singly, but they seem to have come with unusual severity on Mr. Fred Rawlins, formerly train dispatcher here. Just after his resignation, his wife dislocated her ankle, and all three of his bright little children were taken down with scarlet fever. Kitty died, and, owing to the contagious nature of the disease was followed to the cemetery by her bereaved parents alone. Zaida and Mellis rallied and were thought out of danger, but this morning the sad news reached us that Mellis, the little boy, is dead. Mr. and Mrs. Rawlins have a host of friends here who sympathize deeply with them in their bereavement.

Charley Richmond's team became frightened while waiting for a train the other night and started to run away. They only got across the street, when they collided with a big lamp post that anchored them. No damage except breaking one of the irons on the end of the tongue, to which the breast straps are fastened.

The sneak thief referred to elsewhere in this issue, has been getting in his work in good shape and is evidently desirous of starting a livery stable. Sunday night he, or some one else, stole a set of harnesses from Mr. Wakefield, another from George Miller and another from H.C. Neilsen. He also took an overcoat from Miller's place.

Wednesday, January 7, 1891—Mr. Brooks, the U.S. signal service officer, hoisted the first signal this morning. It is a white flag indicating clear weather, and being hoisted over the Chronicle building, we wish it distinctly understood that the white flag does not apply to the Chronicle but only to the weather.

For those readers who believe alcohol was the only substance used recreationally prior to the drug culture of the 1960s, the next news clipping might be quite surprising. Although a much smaller segment of the population was participating back then, there was apparently a drug problem as long ago as January, 1891. And, contrary to popular opinion of the day, it doesn't appear that the Chinese population had a whole lot to do with the rather large quantity involved in this story. The *Chronicle* headline read, "Opium Smugglers Caught":

(Portland)—The police today arrested Joe Billings and Thomas Collins who had in charge about three hundred pounds of unstamped opium.

Billings and Collins were conveying opium in an express wagon, to a hiding place in a remote part of the city. The opium was turned over to the customs officers.

Nothing could have prepared residents of The Dalles for what was to happen on September 2, 1891. It was one of the fastest, most destructive fires the Gorge has ever seen. It all started at the F.W.A. Skibbe home. Consuming the entire residence, the fire jumped to the Eureka Restaurant and then to the saddlery shop of H.L. Kuck and the Skibbe Saloon, despite the building's brick construction. From there it spread throughout the area below the bluff at mind-boggling speed. One of the most disastrous facets of this fire was the way it almost immediately set itself up to simultaneously burn in three different directions. This three-street spread allowed the inferno to consume virtually everything below the bluff, including the Mays and Pease corner downtown, which was considered to be the city's best block.

There seemed no end to the inferno's appetite as it moved through Second and Third streets, hungrily eating its way through the downtown core that had been the pride of the community. It even consumed Neabach's feed yard. The *Chronicle* describes it in eerie detail:

> The flames swept on Third street to the Court street home of Joshua French, going as far as the George Ruch residence on Fourth street, then sweeping around to Fifth and burning all the buildings on that

The Dalles Fire Chief Charles Frank and his lead volunteer firefighters, about 1895. Photo courtesy Barbara Fenkner.

thoroughfare as far as Union street. The Congregational church was swept by the conflagration. . . . One by one the following edifices fell victim: Residence of Omar Sylvester and W.A. Allaway, dwelling houses west of Madison street; Michell's planing mill, now where the Columbia Lumber company is located; the dwellings on Third and the buildings on Second between Federal and Laughlin streets. During this time destruction was raging from Second street south to the bluff. The E.P. Fitzgerald building, the present site of the First National bank, was soon gutted and Gibbons & MacAllister company's hardware store was wiped out of existence. The two-story stable of William Wiley followed. Then the buildings on Third and Federal streets were engulfed by flames. The three-story Vogt block and theatre were soon a mass of ruins.

Residences fell in rows, leaving blackened trails inside the sidewalks way up to the bluff. Among them were the dwellings of Mr. Roscoe, Griffith, Williams, Mrs. Clark E. Griffith and William Michell, the butcher shop of Chrisman Brothers and the grocery of Chrisman & Corson disappeared. The home of J. Doherty and Adams shoe shop rolled away in smoke and ashes. Then followed the grocery store of A. A. Brown and the First Baptist church. Then the Methodist church and the cottage of F.P. Mays went to destruction. Another line of dwellings was snuffed out after the loss of the Methodist church, concluding with the old building known as The Dalles brewery. Tongues of flame were leaping on Court street from the roofs and soon the residences of Messrs. Corson, John Fitzgerald, Sellers and Gray were laid to ruins. The block south of the old brewery was wiped away, comprising the dwellings of William McCoy, William Glacius and Phillip Willig. To the west of Court street another block was sacrificed. Resolved into smoke and ashes were the homes of D.W. Vause, Mrs. J. Juker, Mrs. George Knaggs, W. Wegnerman and O. Kolneraly and the Congregational church.

Meanwhile, the block between Washington and Court streets on the south side of Third Street was in flames. These buildings comprised the residences of Thomas Kelly, Mrs. Lacey, Frank Hill, A.A. Bonney, the engine house and extensive building of the Columbia Packing company.

On Second street, the McDonald Brothers' saloon, a lodging house adjoining, White's restaurant, Wolff's home, the Max Vogt tenement block, Wingate's brick block, D.W. Edward's art gallery, the Berger, Cathcart and Crowe homes and the Pacific fence works were simply piles of coals. Then followed Filloon Brothers' implement warehouse, the block corner Washington and Second, causing a damage of $65,000.

Buildings on a total of 20 blocks were destroyed by the fire, causing one million dollars worth of damage and claiming two lives. Had the fire started just a short

Early fruit processing in the Hood River Valley. The whole family got into the act, including the beagle. Courtesy of Hood River County Historical Museum.

time later, it might have killed many more people who would have been sound asleep by then. That was of little consolation, though, to friends and families of the two people who did lose their lives. This devastating event would forever after be referred to as "The Great Fire."

As families settled in the Hood River Valley and across the river in the White Salmon area, many had planted orchards. Some were finally producing ever-growing crops of apples and pears; others were soon to mature enough for commercial production. Those families needed to find ways to earn money or obtain products for trade. In many cases, the perfect solution was literally right in the backyard.

Lumber is needed to build homes, and there was no shortage of timber in the Gorge. Many were living on veritable forest land that wasn't classified as such. If they knew someone who wanted to log it, they were not restricted in the amount of timber they could clear around their homes. Nearly every man in the area became his own lumberjack for at least a year. Unfortunately, the tendency of settlers to want to clear their property of trees and the constant need for building supplies combined to create some rather unsightly hillsides until enough time had elapsed to allow regrowth of the timber. This occurred only once in the Gorge. By the early twentieth century, planned conservation and reforestation were no longer options open to commercial timber operations, they had become legal mandates.

If a man needed work during the last three decades of the century and didn't mind backbreaking, dangerous jobs, there was plenty of employment to be found in the timber and milling industries. By the 1890s there was a mill on every available body of water along the Columbia, Deschutes, Hood, and White Salmon rivers. Mills in the Gorge not only had to provide lumber for their own communities, but also for the more desolate settlements further upriver.

This did not escape the notice of Jonah H. Mosier, an 1852 Oregon Trail traveler and one of the earliest permanent settlers of the Columbia Gorge. At that time, according to an old (undated) news clipping, there were just two buildings in the entire Gorge (both in The Dalles) and "residences" were tents. Mosier looked around to find the best possible location and decided to build his sawmill on a piece of land 16 miles west of The Dalles, strategically based between what would become Dalles City (The Dalles) and Hood River. By 1854, he had erected the first mill in the area at the mouth of what has since been known as Mosier Creek.

The mill was certainly busy enough to make the Mosier family a great deal of money, but after it was washed out by three spring freshets in four years, Jonah abandoned the mill operations. Several others in the Gorge took up where he left off and by the 1890s there were mills operating on both sides of the Columbia.

Chamberlain sawmill on Rock Creek, Mosier. Horses were used outside the mill, but steam engines were used to power the saws inside. Contributed by Penny Kennedy.

After the fire decimated such a large portion of The Dalles in 1891, families throughout the Gorge benefitted greatly from the close proximity of the timber. It would require an enormous community-wide effort to rebuild the entire downtown district of The Dalles. But these were pioneers, as you'll recall, and they weren't about to be beaten by fire. Lumberjacks and their apprentices worked overtime in the fall and again in the spring of 1892, harvesting all the timber they could during daylight hours, as it was a race against the seasons. Autumn comes early in the Cascade mountains and winter is right on its heels. The first snow would fall in the mountains just days after the fire. Every available man would be needed for labor while it was still possible to access the forest.

Lumberjack operations of the 1890s functioned much like the crew pictured on the cover of this book: several sturdy men took a few horses, several oxen, a couple of wagons, and several two-man hand saws up on the hillside and hollered "tim-berrrr!" to warn the rest of the crew when a tree was falling. When the wagons were full, they took the felled trees to a mill and unloaded them. The mill worked them into proper form—quite different than today's "proper form"—and shipped it out to builders and stores. Proper form in the 1890s ranged from whole logs, grouped with others of similar diameter and length for constructing a log house, to rough finished planks. Until more sophisticated planers made their way west, a "finished" plank closely resembled what we now call "seconds."

Lumberjacks also had the option to work independently and sell heating wood directly to merchants. In the 1890s, the going merchant rate was $1.25 per cord of wood cut and another $1.25 for each cord delivered to the dock. A merchant who purchased a cord for $2.50 sold it for $10 in The Dalles. Not a bad profit.

Local men accomplished an impressive amount of wood-cutting that fall, but of course it wasn't possible to reconstruct all of the burned buildings in The Dalles before winter's chill fell over the valley. Area families shared their homes that winter with those who no longer had one, and many businesses were completely shut down for the better part of a year. Some entrepreneurs were not able to recover from their losses, resulting in the permanent closure of those businesses.

Some new residents didn't have the patience or time to wait for the property to be logged. Ironically, in the years immediately prior to the big fire in The Dalles, the hillside timber had become a nuisance to a man on the other side of the river. Captain Howard C. Cook had filed a claim just west of White Salmon in 1888 and soon discovered he literally couldn't see the forest for the trees. If he had taken time to cut down all the timber and sell it, he estimated that he might not live long enough to see the land cleared for his new home. After trying a variety of ways to cut at least part of the trees out of the way, he finally resorted to setting his acreage on fire, burning a large part of it to create the desired clearing.

The economy shifted a bit that year in the Gorge. Men had to be versatile to provide for their families. The women of the community cared for their neighbors' families and worked feverishly through the winter to make new household linens for their burned-out friends. Yet, in a strange sort of way, the fire boosted parts of

A surreal sight greeted the many who ventured out in rowboats during the 1894 flood. At least half the local population in The Dalles and Hood River plus the entire town of Bingen had nothing else to do while the river was at flood stage. High water marks can still be found on many local buildings. Courtesy of Barbara Coles.

the economy that had been lagging. New sawmills were built to handle the additional construction projects necessitated by the fire and the timber industry were busier than ever. With a nationwide economic depression in full swing at the time, any sort of booming business was welcome news to local residents. The fire could never be looked at as a good thing to have happened, but in keeping with their pioneer grit, the community at large found ways to prosper from a disaster.

If the fire had been the only obstacle in their way that decade, things would have gotten back to normal in a matter of years. Unfortunately, Mother Nature had other plans. When disaster struck just three years later, it directly affected the entire Gorge community and those well beyond, on either side of the river. The most devastating flood the Columbia River had ever produced, perhaps since the natural Bridge of the Gods gave way in ancient history, ravaged the Gorge in late May and early June 1894.

Deep snow had accumulated in the mountains in the winter of 1883–1884. Spring moisture levels that year caught the attention of the area's weather monitors as early as March. Heavy rains fell throughout the Pacific Northwest, causing early melting of the immense mountain snow pack. One 20-year resident said he had never seen so much snow locally, some 18 feet on the level and as much as 60 feet deep in the canyons. Spring run-off normally beginning its descent in early May had already increased the Columbia's volume substantially by the end of March, causing washouts along both the Snake and Columbia Rivers. Newspaper articles noted rock slides at Mosier and Hood River that stopped train traffic.

In early May, residents began to feel a sense of relief as temperatures dropped and the Columbia receded a bit, but by mid-month it was on the rise again. It was becoming evident the river would reach its annual high-water mark well ahead of schedule at the end of June. Between May 19 and 21, the rain began to fall again, raising the river's level by 1 to 2 feet every 24-hour period. May 24 brought a welcome burst of sunshine, but went to the extreme with a 98 degree day that drew even more moisture from the snow pack and down the mountainsides. Although the *Times-Mountaineer* editorial assured readers that in 1882 city streets had been raised above the 1876 flood levels (51 feet 3 inches on June 23), merchants along Front Street in The Dalles began moving inventory out of their cellars the following day when the Columbia was measured at 41 feet.

May 26 brought more rain and telegraph poles washed out along the railroad. With the river at 49 feet by May 28, nobody held out much hope of staying dry. Train service between Hood River and The Dalles was halted because the tracks were washing out, and merchants on Second Street in The Dalles were moving their goods to higher ground. Across the river in Bingen, families were doing the same. They didn't have long to wait before realizing the magnitude of the coming flood. The very next day found people boating Union and Court streets, railroad

An insecure track is all that remained of the elevated railroad trestle running parallel to Lincoln Street. This photo was taken by Father Alphonse Bronsgeest after the water had receded several feet, as can be seen in the high water marks on St. Mary's academy (right). Part of Umatilla House can be seen on the far left, with the Columbia Hotel immediately to its right. Courtesy of The Dalles Chronicle.

tracks completely submerged, Mill Creek washed out, and the canneries losing fish wheels to the rising river. The Umatilla House was providing free boat rides to both visitors and locals, playing on the romantic theme of similar vessels in Venice, Italy. On May 31, the Columbia was measured at 53 feet, 6 inches —already 2 feet above the 1876 high water mark and still rising. All railroad service east of Portland was halted, people were rafting from one location to another in The Dalles, and several houses and outbuildings from upstream drifted downriver through the Gorge.

Gorge press rooms were flooded out during the first week of June. The first newspaper back in operation was the *Times-Mountaineer* in The Dalles on June 4, followed by *the Chronicle* on the 13th. *The Chronicle* building flooded badly. The first *Times-Mountaineer* issue printed after onset of the flood reported the Columbia River currently at 57 feet, 10 inches and rising. Prisoners were removed from the city's jail when the water was a foot deep in the cells. Businesses in the flood's path continued to move valuable inventory to higher ground, although some had given up the fight due to lack of alternative locations. On June 5, Union Pacific Railroad began a series of attempts to send a steamboat over the flooded falls on the river. The "Harvest Queen" nearly made it upriver, but was foiled when it wrecked on a boulder despite the river reaching its astounding all-time record level of 59 feet, 9 inches on June 6. Observers were greeted with the surreal

A sad overview of the destruction caused by the 1894 flood, this photo was taken from northeast The Dalles. Houses are literally consumed by the river, and freight cars sit atop submerged rails while the trestles drift away into the river. Courtesy of Barbara Coles.

sight and sounds of several houses, barns, and outbuildings being carried on the current. More than one barn came downriver with a rooster crowing and chickens clucking from its rooftop, seeming to announce its trip out to sea.

Many frame houses and a few businesses based in the Gorge were completely washed away by the flood waters before they began to recede on June 7. The local Chinese community was among the hardest hit, since a large portion of their homes were standard "immigrant shanties" located near the river's edge. For 16 days, the Columbia flowed at an excess of a million cubic feet per second, peaking on June 6 at 1.2 million cubic feet. Sadly, the area of The Dalles that was burned out in 1891 was also one of the areas hardest hit by the flood. Other towns in the Gorge that took the brunt of the damage included Columbus (now known as Maryhill), Grants, and Bingen. Hood River's damage was less direct since most of the town was above the flood plain, but the local strawberry crop, lacking transportation to the outside marketplace, literally rotted. Loss to the strawberry growers was estimated at $40,000.

One family living in Columbus moved their valuables to the attic and evacuated their home, staying with friends downriver in Cascade Locks. One can only imagine their shock when they saw their entire home float by a short time later. A distillery at Grants, which was located at the foot of a cliff between Rufus and Biggs, was set adrift during the flood. The building was spotted by ferry operator Lucias Clark and, with the help of a fellow by the name of McDonald, rowed out and coaxed the building to shore. Several barrels of aged whiskey bobbed their way downstream, tempting many a drinking man past the point of good sense. Two such men were George Rankin and George Purser. According to one newspaper article, they were "tantalized to the point of desperation" and rowed out to rope one of the kegs, only to be defeated by the swift current.

Although The Dalles businesses were hard hit and the new wooden sidewalks downtown (that had been rebuilt after the 1891 fire) had literally been taken out to sea, local residents had one big thing to be thankful for—not a single human life was lost as a direct result of the flood. And although Seuferts, Winans and Halls lost several fish wheels to the flood, when the fish were able to make their way upstream again in mid-June, an unprecedented number of salmon chose to use one of Seufert's remaining fish wheels. The result was a record canning season that brought enough excess income to purchase replacement fish wheels. The Dalles became a city of tents and wooden shacks that bore a close resemblance to mining towns of earlier decades across Oregon. The Dalles National Bank even set up shop in a tent, offering banking services from that location beginning two days after the floodwaters crested.

A great many treasures, both large and small, were destroyed by the flood. One of the most tragic losses involved the Umatilla House, a building located at the corner of First and Union streets, whose history already ran deeper and longer than almost any other structure in the Gorge. Although it wasn't completely destroyed by the flood, the damage was so extensive that this icon of Western success never fully recovered from its losses.

The first Umatilla House was built in 1857 by A.J. Nixon and purchased in 1860 by Daniel Handley and N.B. Sinnott. From the beginning it was designed and run as a first-class establishment, while hosting numerous groups of "common folk" as well. The charming, well-run hotel quickly became known across the nation as the finest establishment west of Chicago and north of San Francisco. From its architecture to the furniture and fixtures, the Umatilla House had a character and grace that spoke to all who visited.

Yet it wasn't just its aesthetics that appealed to such a wide array of people. Management was extremely efficient, yet completely gracious. Employees were professional, yet friendly. The combination was difficult enough to find in more established parts of the country; it was unheard of in the outback of the West.

The owners made it a point to never allow stocks to become low, for doing so could be a death knoll on the frontier. It was not uncommon to find as much as 2,500 gallons of whiskey on hand and a cellar full of eggs, beef, and ham. Meats were purchased by the ton rather than the pound and entire garden crops of local farmers were bought to keep patrons happily consuming their vegetables. Strawberries and wild berries of the region were served early on and, when local orchards had matured in later years, pears, apples, and peaches were also utilized in the dining room. And of course there was plenty of fresh trout, salmon, and sturgeon in summer and fall. The dining room itself was a study in good living, with its beautiful décor and seating for 250 people.

Even the barroom was elaborately decorated. Regional meetings of stockmen, grain growers, orchardists, and even the military were often held here. It was also the preferred location for high-stakes poker. With its own private carriage functioning as the era's equivalent of today's airport shuttle, the Umatilla House was the darling of the Pacific Northwest.

In addition to local residents who enjoyed having a night of elegance and opulence now and again, the hotel hosted many guests during its many years of operation, both distinguished and wayward. Used at times as an overflow facility for the jail, its early records reveal the stays of a few prisoners along with such notables as President Ulysses S. Grant, Vice President Schuyler Colfax, General William Tecumseh Sherman, several senators, authors Rudyard Kipling and Mark Twain, Railroad magnate Henry Villard, a list of professional boxers, and even well-known inventor Thomas Alva Edison and his wife.

The life of the Umatilla House was not always one of fine dining and gracious living. It suffered several tragic events including two devastating fires; the second time, in 1879, it burned to the ground. On both occasions it was rebuilt, only to be damaged again by the destructive flood of 1894. As floodwaters encroached upon the historic structure, owners Sinnott and Fish created a false floor high above the ground floor restaurant and cooked the restaurant meals in their private upstairs residence, creating a haven for the displaced residents as well as a meeting place for anyone who just happened to be out rowing around. However, the losses suffered proved too much to fully recover from. The once proud hotel fell into disrepair during the early 1900s and was ordered destroyed by its third and final owner, H.B. Salisbury, on June 30, 1930.

Several items from within the hotel remain in the community to this day, including some of the bar stools, a stair banister, deck chairs, and a bride's mirror. Many other artifacts are intact but no longer belong to anyone living in the Gorge area. As a measure of the community's respect for the grand lady of the Northwest, a Umatilla House carriage still travels the local parade circuit.

Pioneer Jonah Mosier died in 1894. His son Jefferson bought out his siblings and used the family's original 320-acre Donation Land Claim parcel to plat the town of Mosier. A number of settlers had lived in the surrounding area for a number of years, but the town hadn't been platted. The first commercial establishment (aside from the defunct mill) was a store and ticket office built by J.J. Lynch when the railroad came through in 1882. Situated directly opposite the tracks, it also served as the post office.

Progress was slowed but not halted by fire and water in the 1890s. As new technology created opportunity, it was embraced without hesitation—a philosophy still generally true today. Salmon canneries sprang up and fruit operations also became increasingly automated. The Seufert family's cannery in The Dalles was already producing 1,500 cases of salmon per day in 1896, despite the national economic depression prevailing from 1893 to 1897.

One small settlement along the river on the Oregon side was especially prosperous during the 1890s. Then known as Whiskey Flat, this community had grown from an isolated settlement of just a handful of people—three white families and a small group of Klickitat Indians in 1853—to a viable village of roughly 1,000 in 1893. In the early 1890s Whiskey Flat was anything but lifeless.

The Umatilla House suffered the flood, but the upper floor was a haven for locals with no other place to go. Balcony parking, of course. Courtesy of The Dalles Chronicle.

People were living in everything from shacks and lean-to type structures to tents. They were there to build the Cascade Locks, which would allow large boats to come upstream through one of the worst sections of the Columbia. Boats would be moved through a series of gated locks to bring them past the rocky rapids in a manner similar to the famous canal built a short time later in Panama. This construction operation required a large number of workers with a wide range of skills—everything from stone cutters and masons to carpenters, iron workers, and explosives experts. The few years the project was in progress, it became a true "wild west" community with the primary businesses being saloons and traders. The name "Whiskey Flat" was coined due to the feverish consumption of alcoholic beverages by the workmen (presumably during their off-work hours) of the new locks.

No churches or religious meetings existed in Whiskey Flat until a stonecutter by the name of William Hoskins came to town. However, the arrival of a religious outlet did little to quell the drinking problem. It was a problem that would be solved gradually, as the locks were completed and the hamlet became a bona fide hometown, known as Cascade Locks. R.G. O'Connor, a river diver, served as Superintendent of Gates at the new locks.

The opening of this engineering feat paved the way for easier settlement upriver and fortified the resolve of many who wanted to reside in close proximity to the locks.

Despite the disastrous way the decade began, not all was negative. In fact, those early-in-the-decade losses served as a catalyst for positive change. Many lives were rebuilt along with the construction that took place to replace or repair dwellings and businesses.

8. PACK TRAINS AND STAGECOACHES

A history without some discussion of the freight and stage routes throughout the Gorge simply wouldn't be a complete account. Due to a combination of its central location in the scheme of things and the isolation of early settlers east of the Cascades, this area was a hotbed of activity in terms of transportation. In fact, it still is—minus the old Pony Express and stagecoach runs, of course.

While Wilamette Valley settlers were connected to the rest of the world in a variety of ways, Gorge settlers relied heavily on inland transportation. Likewise, having the longest water channel in the West meant the Gorge had always provided one of the main facilities for water transport.

Although messengers were often dispatched on horseback to deliver important news to a specific destination in the 1850s, there was not an official express service established for that purpose until the Gold Rush of the early 1860s. Likewise, freight drivers were dispatched with teams of pack horses or mules for other types of freight beginning in the late 1850s. A good pack horse could carry up to a 200-pound load of freight. The heavier the total load, the greater the number of horses required to haul it, thus forming the "train." The earliest scheduled pack train service from The Dalles to the mines was operated by J.W. Case, J.J. Cozart, and D.N. Luce. They called themselves "The Knights of Primeval Transportation." Personal travel generally took place on horseback because the terrain was not conducive to wagon travel. Most "roads" were at best trails until the late 1860s. Even then it took a strong constitution to travel by buggy over the rugged back country near the Gorge.

Joseph H. Sherar managed a pack train operation from 1862–1864, running from The Dalles to various mining camps of eastern Oregon and Idaho without incident. He sold his business to Robert Heppner for $6,000. During Heppner's second trip, he lost the entire outfit in a skirmish with Indians.

The Pony Express was added to local choices for transporting freight, small parcels, and correspondence in late 1861 as a result of the Canyon City gold rush. Full-scale Express services got underway in the spring of 1862 when Thomas Brents of Walla Walla established his well-known Pony Express between The

The Concord Coach: not just for Cinderella. This versatile coach was used by Wells Fargo and every other stagecoach company throughout the West until about 1915 for passenger service.

Dalles and Canyon City. He charged 50¢ for a letter and three percent of the value of gold for transport. This was due to the fact that it was one of the most dangerous runs in the West at the time, with long distances between settlements that almost begged bandits and killers to use the opportunity against the express riders.

On a return trip to The Dalles one time, carrying a fair amount of gold, Brents noticed a campfire burning near where he crossed the John Day River. Hoping to camp with the another party as a safety measure, Brents approached the small group at the campfire and asked permission to join them. "Imagine our surprise," he said, "when we looked into the face of Berry Way, the most dreaded outlaw of the west, who with his wife and a man had murdered a man on the Ochoco." The outlaws of course welcomed Brents and, unaware he recognized them, inquired whether he was carrying a lot of treasure. Carelessly throwing his pack to the ground, Brents responded, "No, it's only mule shoes this time for a big pack train just coming in down the river," and went about his business that evening, pretending to completely ignore the bag. When he bedded down that night he made sure the pack was in full view and his hand was on his pistol beneath the blanket. He pretended to sleep but kept constant watch over it all night. None the wiser about his knowledge, the bandits allowed him to ride off unharmed the next morning. Berry Way was hanged soon thereafter by vigilantes near Canyon City, eliminating the possibility Brents might ever stumble upon him again. Brents went on to be postmaster at Canyon City and later, a superior court judge in Walla Walla.

Although some large nuggets were found—including a 23.5-ounce specimen that brought great joy to its owner—there was a relatively small quantity at Canyon City and the gold rush there was short-lived. A hard winter in early 1864 brought the Pony Express to a temporary halt in February and the previous year's discovery of gold in other parts of eastern Oregon turned attention permanently away from Canyon City in the spring, reducing the mining population from about 10,000 to less than a thousand. Miners who chose to work as employees, rather than have an unpredictable income while working for themselves, could earn as much as $150 per month by working seven days a week.

Celebrated Oregon poet (Charles) Joaquin Miller was a Pony Express rider long before he was well known for his poetry. The following passages have been excerpted from his comments about the experience:

> Gold was discovered in 1860. I was admitted to the bar before I was 21 so I brought my law book and 2 six-shooters and came out to the gold fields. There was not much gold to be found and nobody was interested in law, so I became a Pony Express rider and Mail Carrier from Walla Walla to Millersburg, Idaho. I rode early and late and almost lived in the saddle as a Pony Express rider between Walla Walla and Grangeville, Idaho. A Lapwai Indian and myself followed the Indian trail across the Craig mountain and Camas Prairie. Idaho in those days was known as E-dah-hoe an Indian word signifying "light on the mountains." I spelled it Idaho in my writings and that may have gave it first use in print.
>
> Our service was simple express carrying service with cheap equipment comparing in no way with the costly and elaborate Pony Express from St. Joe to Sacramento. The job was full of hardships, perils, long riding hours, day and night work in all kinds of weather with desperate as well as good men on the trails. I changed horses from 5 to 10 times daily; rode at desperate speeds using Indian ponies only, without any escort. We called ourselves Mossman & Millers Pony Express. The Indians were numerous but we weren't afraid of them, but of the whites we were. The Indians were peaceful. We hired them to tend our stations. They were of the Nez Perce tribes. California emptied her miners, gamblers, robbers and desperadoes right into our mines and roads thither.

Cayuse ponies were preferred for many purposes entailing extended periods of galloping, because of their compact size and powerful stride. Miller gives us a clear picture of some of the rough characters inhabiting the West in those early days, as well as showing us the youth that powered a lot of the risky ventures undertaken. He takes us on a harrowing ride in the dead of winter:

> The rivers were closed with ice that winter, the Snake [river] being icebound at Lewiston. The miners wanted to get their money and letters to Walla Walla and to friends and families. The snow was deep in the Idaho mountains. The trails were drifted full. It was a question of whether any living man could face those conditions, make that ride and live to tell about it! They asked the Indians to try: they refused to do so. I started out with letters and $10,000 in gold weighing 50 pounds, to

Walla Walla. Dave English and Boone Helm, two California desperados, followed me with the evident intention of robbing and possibly killing me for the gold I carried. I noted Canada Joe, worst of the killers of the west, far ahead of me up the trail, in the blizzard.

I was able to keep ahead of my pursuers. The problem was to get around Canada Joe. He had 3 six-shooters strapped around him. I knew he would use them. Our horses continued to flounder up the mountain. I noted Joe was heading for a blocked off narrow place in the trail to make his stand against my approach. I couldn't turn back as English and Helm were back there in that blizzard and couldn't be eluded. I noted ahead, where the trail levelled off, that I was nearing the top of the mountain, so I struck out in a new direction. Canada Joe seen this and opened fire on me but his chilled hands and body were too unsteady. His bullets whizzed about us but we were soon lost in the blizzard and made good time on top of the mountain and down the other side. We eluded our pursuer and made it safely to Walla Walla.

One very short freight transportation era that came before the stagecoach days should never be allowed to be lost in the annals of history. It was a very creative endeavor, though probably not very well thought out prior to its implementation. It was, if you can believe it, the "Camel Express." Yes, camels were the animals of choice for a pack train route in 1859. Although it had its terminus slightly beyond the Columbia Gorge, a fair amount of Gorge freight was carried by camel that year because the route connected with pack trains originating in The Dalles.

By this thin thread, it qualifies for inclusion in this discussion, if preservation of a great story isn't enough. And as strange as it sounds, a lot of logic went into the choice of camels. It was largely in desert country, running about 700 miles over the Mullen trail from Walla Walla in Washington Territory to Virginia City, Montana. Another Camel Express route ran from Umatilla to the Bannock mines in Idaho, also covering a large amount of desert country. The scarcity of water, the need to pack heavier loads to minimize the frequency of these trips, and the number of stops made camels a logical choice.

The part probably not so well planned was the camels' need for enormous amounts of food compared to a horse, which was an expensive proposition in the West where supplies were often scarce. Winter was an especially difficult time to obtain necessary items, which drove up feed costs considerably. Another problem encountered was the reaction of other animals at the sight of a camel on the trail. Some horses and mules were so frightened they stampeded or broke completely away from the pack train, causing damage to the freight or losing it entirely. It must have been a lot like seeing an alien lumbering down the path! After a very short burst of business, the teams of $1,200 imported Asian camels were replaced by horse- and mule-drawn wagons.

The name of Ben Holliday will be familiar to many readers as one of the early icons of stagecoach service. In 1862 he purchased the St. Joseph, Missouri, to

Sacramento, California, route from Russell, Majors & Waddell. Less than two years later, Holliday upgraded and expanded the service to points in Idaho. He bought a fleet of new coaches and staffed the entire run with the best drivers and fastest livestock he could locate, leasing sections of the route to several subcontractors. The advertising for his empire boasted service to Placerville, California, with connections to The Dalles, Umatilla, Walla Walla, and Fort Hall. The weekly Fort Hall-to-The Dalles runs were contracted to John Hailey and Henry Greathouse, soon spurring creation of a little empire when they formed a partnership that bought out competitor Thomas Express & Stage Company. At that point they held the contracts for all mail and passenger service between The Dalles and Fort Hall, raking in the princely contract fee of $80,000 per year. Service became daily in 1866.

Holliday's Overland Stage Line from Salt Lake City to Boise made its first run during that same period, arriving August 11, 1864, to create a full-circle connection linking Salt Lake City, Boise, The Dalles, Sacramento, and intermediate stops along the way. Cost for the average passenger was prohibitive at $1,000 per round trip, but that was the beginning of mobility throughout the West. Each added route also made the mail move faster between points. The roads were still horrible then, but the stage company attempted to compensate by using the Cinderella-style Concord coaches when weather permitted it, and the more durable mud-wagon style carriages when conditions were, well—muddy.

Henry H. Wheeler (for whom Wheeler County was named) established the first stage route through Canyon City from The Dalles in 1864, despite the lack of real

Just south of Antelope, this freight team is contracted by the Shaniko, Bend and Silver Lake Fast Freight company. The 10-horse team is headed down Antelope Creek at the foot of Cow Canyon near Cross Keys, towards the junction with the Canyon City wagon road. Courtesy of The Dalles Chronicle.

roads. He used four-horse coaches, changing them six to eight times over the course of each run. He had the mail contract, as well as the Wells Fargo "Fast Express" contract. The Wells Fargo coaches carried only mail, a shotgun guard, and no passengers. Twice-weekly passenger service was established on August 15, 1864.

A resident of the isolated village of Mitchell along the Pony Express route to Canyon City, Wheeler was already familiar with the freighting end of the business and the need for changing the horses at several points along the way. He undoubtedly knew the route well and had seen the potential of owning the stagecoach route and being able to also own one of the stage stops. Unfortunately for him, he was probably also thinking the new military road would soon be built, causing much less wear and tear on the buggies. In that respect he may have been disappointed to discover what kind of "road building" was actually performed on the road (see Chapter 5). But the road crew did at least move the large rocks out of the road.

The Canyon City run largely followed the original pioneer trail and sections of the old Indian trails. The stage left from the Umatilla House, each coach carrying as many as six passengers. In the earliest years, the area between The Dalles and Canyon City was so sparsely populated that the only stage stops were at Sherar's Bridge, Maupin's Station (near where Antelope now stands), a place called Burnt Ranch on the John Day River, and another at Mitchell.

By today's standards it would be ridiculous to stop every 30-50 miles on a 180-mile trip, but if one considers that it took two and a half days to complete the run back then, three or four stops hardly seems unreasonable. The $80 round-trip fare must have seemed rather steep to a passenger who had to endure two and a half

Wapinitia store and Post Office, one of the stage stops, in its heyday. Courtesy of The Dalles Chronicle.

days of bumping over the trail, with several hours of torture between stops. The pioneers were tough in a lot of ways we don't normally realize.

Other stage routes of the 1860s included The Dalles to Umatilla, The Dalles to Walla Walla, and The Dalles to Montana. With the exception of the Canyon City run, all eastbound stage routes followed the same path almost as far as Walla Walla. Henry Ward apparently felt he had a secret to making good time from one point to another (or he wanted the public to believe he had one), because he even went so far as to advertise it as the "air line route of 80 miles" in 1867 issues of *The Dalles Times-Mountaineer*. His run was between The Dalles and Umatilla Landing at the time, but was later expanded 45 miles to terminate in Walla Walla.

A surprisingly small percentage of all stage drivers lost their lives as a direct result of their work, although many life-threatening injuries were incurred. The job would have merited the highest possible rating for hazards if pioneers had already established industrial insurance as we have it now, perhaps exceeded only by rates merited for Pony Express riders of the earliest days. Between runaway animals, narrow ledges on the trail, Indian conflicts, and good old-fashioned bad guys trying to rob every courier, it seems illogical that any of them at all survived. Even the simplest problem could end in death, similar to the case of John Turner, who drove one of the early Dalles-to-Walla Walla routes. This snippet from the October 23, 1868 issue of the *Times-Mountaineer* says it all: "John Turner, driver on The Dalles to Walla Walla stage, whose outfit upset going down John Day Hill, died of injuries received last week."

Shortly after Ben Holliday sold his interests in the Overland Stage Lines, C.M. Lockwood became a transportation mogul. In 1868, he was able to bid just low enough to receive the Wells Fargo contracts for the Canyon City, Walla Walla, and Salt Lake City routes. He made a massive amount of money, but tried to do too much of the work himself, resulting in serious medical problems that forced him to sub-contract an extra section to John Hailey only halfway through his contract period. Lockwood's health was so severely compromised that he died in early 1873 at the age of just 38 years. Hailey, on the other hand, had started with Holliday in the early 1860s, fulfilled Lockwood's contract in 1870, and then operated the same route until 1874 as a contractor to Northwest Stage Company. Hailey was probably the longest-running contractor in the Northwest during that time frame.

Transportation remained much the same throughout the 1870s. The main changes were increases in frequency for many of the stage routes and the addition of or changes to routes originally run some distance away from where the numerous short-line railroads were springing up. By connecting water routes with stage routes and stage routes with railroad lines, a significant amount of time could be saved on freight and regular mail transportation. The savings became even more pronounced as the transcontinental railroad lines were completed in the early 1880s.

So many contractors and drivers worked for short periods from 1870–1914 that it is nearly impossible to track them all down. Hugh Jackson had the longest lasting contract for The Dalles-Shaniko-Canyon City and The Dalles-Wapinitia runs. The Shaniko, Bend and Silver Lake Fast Freight company operated a north-south route connecting with Jackson's. Another run went through Sand Springs (near where Biggs now lies) and then south to connect to the other lines at Maupin's stage stop near Antelope. The Dalles-Shaniko stage was a popular one with the locals during the late 1800s and early 1900s. The Dalles to Canyon City run disbanded in 1910, having become somewhat obsolete as a result of the railroad's completion. The run from The Dalles to Wapinitia continued until 1914, making an occasional charter to Crook County and beyond as required. Concord carriages were used when stage traffic was heavy and two-horse "hacks" in lighter traffic.

Jess M. Gray served first as a stage driver for Hugh Jackson, and soon thereafter saved enough money to buy his own stage, freight wagon, and team so he could subcontract the services from Jackson. Jess started his career as a stage driver at age 16, first taking the run from The Dalles to Shaniko. After acquiring his own stage and team to pull it, he took over the run between The Dalles and Canyon City in the fall and winter, operating his own freight line from Shaniko to Bend and sometimes beyond in summer. Toward the end of the stagecoach era, Gray's fall and winter run took him from the Umatilla House down through eight-mile, Boyd, Nansene, Chicken Springs, Keen, Shearar's Bridge, Flanagan, Bakeoven, and finally to Shaniko. From Shaniko, G.M. Cornett took the run to Antelope, Burnt Ranch, Ashwood, and finally to Mitchell. Another contractor took it from there to Canyon City.

The Dalles to Shaniko stagecoach run was 58 miles. In good weather, it could be made by one driver with a single team of hard-working horses. It was a long, dusty trail in summer. In fall and winter, it alternated between muddy and slick with snow or ice, but it was always cold. Jess Gray related to family members how he had to bundle up in sheepskin clothing, and even then the chill would settle into his bones, permeate his entire body, and numb his limbs. It was simply a way of life for Jess back then (and many others whose work took them outdoors). Upon arrival at either his final destination or a way point, the driver still needed to tend his horses or mules, eat his own dinner, and bed down for the night. He usually slept under the stars, often sleeping under the wagon itself in wet weather, when there were no accommodations to be found in the barn or if valuable freight required a full-time guard.

Because of the cold weather and nasty conditions, Jess and the other veteran stage drivers learned many tricks enabling them to minimize their exposure to the elements. One of these was the way they picked up and delivered the smaller freight parcels that were transferred at individual ranches.

Pouches resembling socks were tied to the gates of each ranch or property that had outgoing freight or mail. A veteran stage driver could lasso one of these socks with his carriage whip, without ever getting up from his seat. Gray, among other seasoned drivers, would wrap his blacksnake whip around the sock and draw it over to the stage without so much as stopping. He was also known for being able to cut a rattlesnake in two with his whip at distances up to 12 feet (a good, safe distance from a rattler), never allowing the team to break stride. He held an exemplary record as a driver, never having wrecked a single stage, even in the wicked winter weather.

As the last of the pioneer stage coach and freight wagon drivers alive in the area by the 1940s, Gray recalled in an interview shortly before his death:

> At times our passenger list contained some pretty hard-looking men, but I was never held up or molested. On the freighting runs to Prineville, Burns, Silver Lake, Bend or Lakeview, I generally hauled merchandise, farm supplies, machinery, lumber, nails, liquor and clothing. No runs were made for any particular outfit or business concern. On the return trips we brought back wool, hides, wheat, meat and other farm products.
>
> It was hard work, always away from home, exposed to all types of weather, muddy and boggy roads, snow, ice or dust, breakdowns, sick horses, broken harnesses, wagons or equipment; wagons sliding off the road; dry camps without water, sleeping out under the stars; poor food or none at all; run-away teams which would break up the wagons and scatter the merchandise. It was a hard life even when conditions were at their best. Most of the drivers were hard drinkers of bad liquor and lived short lives.

Jess Gray, the last stage & freight driver known to be living in the Gorge in the 1940s, posed for this photo in front of his home earlier that century. Courtesy of Gray family archives.

Though he was "never held up or molested" on his stage or freight runs, Jess did encounter some of the worst of the worst men of his time shortly after the stage runs ceased entirely in 1914. While out on a contract run for a business client, he was taken captive by some of Pancho Villa's men and learned a great deal about their operations in the western states during that time. He provided enough detail to an interested nephew to later allow him to locate one of the caves used by Villa's men between New Mexico and Oregon.

Other stage drivers and their routes, where known, are listed below for routes originating in the Gorge or connecting with local routes. Years of birth and death or dates of service are in parenthesis if known. That is followed by a short list of local Wells Fargo Express agents, with the company name if known. The third is a list of stage stations, showing their owners/operators where known and noting the presence of a hotel where applicable. These lists were gathered from a variety of sources and are considered to be reliable for these purposes, but by no means should either list be considered exhaustive or confirmed.

Drivers included: Harry Adams, stage and freight operator; Justin Chenoweth (Chenowith/Chenoweth Creek named for him); Hank Monk; Baldy Green; Billy Hamilton; Clark Foss; Buck Jones; Chas. McConnell; "Buffalo Jim" Geiser; Bob Hill; Henry Ward; Buck Montgommery; Hill Beachy; Bob Geiser; George Quimsby; Dave Horn; William Ellis; C.W. Barger; Tom Vaughn; William Glover; Gus Freeman; Dave Wright; John Gleeson; George Richards; Jerry Crowder; Jack Gillman; Chas. Hines; Wm. Lockwood; Jesse Gray; Jonathan Patterson; Wm. Theelman; Big Bill Lockwood; Samuel Rufus Cox (Antelope to Mitchell), still driving 1904; Thomas Ward (1846–1903), Canyon City route until 1876; Mr. Kelly, The Dalles to Wapinitia 1901.

Governor Zenith Moody was the agent for Wells Fargo; Robert B. Reed (d. 1888—married to Mary J. Davis) was an early agent for Wells Fargo, also Wasco Company Clerk in the early days.

Stage stops on the Oregon side of the Gorge included Fairbanks; Dechutesville/Miller); Biggs; Samuel & Palmyra Price—Price's Station at Sand Spring at the head of Price's Canyon, south of Biggs near Highway 206; the Pratts at 11-Mile House near Boyd; Thomas Ward (1846–1903) on the Long Hollow Road at Nansene post-1876 (hotel); Chicken Springs; Keen; Sherar's Bridge (hotel); Flanagan; Andy Swift Bakeoven (hotel); Shaniko (1900—also hotel); John Ward (father of Thomas) at Maupin Station; Antelope; Leonard's Bridge (later Scott's Ferry) at the Oregon Trail Crossing of the John Day River; Daniel Leonard's, due east of Wasco; Rock Creek (5–8 miles south of Arlington); Willow Creek/Cecil; Wells Springs; Hewitt's or Huott's at Eight-Mile; Dufur (hotel); Wapinitia.

In October of 1871, Joseph Shearer (former pack train operator) left his stock raising operation in Tygh Valley and purchased the property that would become known as Sherar's Bridge, on the Deschutes River rapids. There he took out the original rickety foot bridge present since 1826 and erected a solid wooden structure fit for wagon passage. The bridge was built at great expense, resulting in it being operated as a toll bridge for many years thereafter. According to at least one account, Sherar built a small hotel when he first settled, constructing a fine, 33-room hotel on the west bank in 1893.

Mrs. Sherar (Jane A. Herbert) decorated and furnished the hotel in grand style, taking advantage of every modern convenience available. The hotel faced the Deschutes rapids and looked out on rolling hills; its grounds included a small, spring-fed orchard and garden that produced fruits and vegetables needed for feeding guests. The property was managed by family members until it burned to the ground as a result of a stray cinder thrown by a passing steam engine around 1940.

Finally, what would a wild western town have been without its own Miss Kitty? The Dalles had its own version along with many of the usual saloon-side attractions found in old western movies. In this case, her name was Katherine "Kitty" Bice, the daughter of Sidney and Margaret Bice. At one point she was married to Bruce "Smokey" Houston and had a son named Alan. She "managed" the Blue Goose Saloon—and its brothel.

Eventually convicted of killing a man, she was sentenced to five years in prison. Family lore has it that her family was so ashamed they moved to the Oregon coast to get away from the scene of the ordeal. One can't help wondering just what Miss Kitty used to kill her victim. But we can be relatively sure it wasn't kindness.

The famous hotel at Sherar's Bridge, about 1900, which burned down in 1940 when a cinder from a passing train landed on the roof. The toll bridge spanned the Deschutes River. Sam Gates is the gentleman driving the cart. Courtesy of The Dalles Chronicle.

9. War, Prohibition, Automation, and Modernization

The first two decades of the twentieth century were filled with a dizzying array of major advances worldwide. Transportation received a huge shot in the arm with the invention of the airplane and integration of the automobile into modern society. Many areas in the western states were using electricity to light local businesses and homes. These innovations may have had a greater impact on society than others prior to the personal computer. On the negative side World War I, tuberculosis, and a deadly influenza collectively claimed many lives worldwide. Gorge residents shared both good and bad with the rest of the globe, but they also had many of their own major victories, celebrations, and even some special legislation. It was an amazingly busy time.

The spring of 1900 was an exceptionally wet one. A March 29 article in *The Dalles Chronicle* quotes Jim Gray of Victor (near Wapinitia, a distance south of The Dalles):

> I have lived 33 years in eastern Oregon and I have never seen the soil so well saturated with moisture nor the grain crop so full of promise of a big harvest as they are at this moment. I have 300 acres sown to fall wheat that looks as fine as any I ever saw in my life.

Gray continues, saying there was a hard frost on Wapinitia flat the night before, and he feared for the viability of the fruit crop as a result. As was the custom of the day, the article goes on to say "However, Jim never worries himself about crossing bridges before he comes up against them. He is a sound money Democrat, has a healthy liver, trusts in God, reads the *Chronicle*, and votes the Republican ticket." Unfortunately for Mr. Gray, his liver wasn't where the focus should have been when he was watching his health.

The next article to appear in the newspaper about Mr. Gray was printed on July 14 of the same year, a little less than four months after the first. It said,

> Yesterday afternoon, about 1 o'clock, James Gray, whose home is on Juniper Flat near Victor, started out from this city with a new $3,000 threshing outfit, bound for Dufur, where he had a great deal of

threshing to do. Reaching Eight-Mile about 5 p.m. and finding Mrs. Huott unable to prepare supper for them, they secured a meal about a half mile beyond and returning, made their bed out near the barn.

In fact, the threshing outfit was purchased as a direct result of the fabulous wheat crop soon to be sown throughout the county due to the wet spring season they experienced. The crop looked so "full of promise" Gray decided to gamble a bit and buy the first fully-automated threshing outfit east of the Cascades, then contract his services out to fellow wheat ranchers to sow their crops quickly. Quite a big deal was made of this new-fangled equipment when Gray and his employees and family members went to get it in The Dalles. A photo was taken in front of the W.A. Johnston store to commemorate the event, complete with some sort of large framed certificate. The *Chronicle* then stated:

Mr. Gray was apparently well when they went to bed at 8:30, save a slight pain in his breast, which they thought little of. About four o'clock this morning Mr. Payne, whom he slept with, got up and Gray asked him for a drink, when he was handed a cup of water. He again spoke of the pain in his chest, but as he often had slight pains of that sort, little heed was given it. The man [Payne] returned to bed and about five o'clock arose, when he found Gray was lying there dead. In a short time

James J. Gray (on machinery to the left of the men holding the commemorative plaque) and his entourage depart The Dalles with the first fully-automated threshing outfit east of the Cascades, July 13, 1900. Courtesy of Gray family photo archives.

the coroner was sent for, and in company with the recorder and undertaker went out there and held an inquest.

The article continues, stating Gray was a man of about 65 years of age who left a wife (Susan Hurst Gray) and several young children. The inquest concluded he died of an apparent heart attack. His widow and children ran their wheat farm and contracted with other farmers for thresher use in an attempt to finish paying for the equipment, but Mrs. Gray was duped by "Doc" Covey, who was trusted with managing the farm operations. He soon married her, then found so many ways to pay himself and his brother for "services" that almost nothing was left of the estate when the farm was sold and closed its doors nine years later. When the widow had proof of the embezzlement, she packed his belongings and threw them out in front of the house in his absence, then gave him the option of leaving town or facing her wrath in court. Covey immediately departed for Canada and she filed for a quiet divorce. As far as anyone knows, he never returned to the Columbia Gorge.

This was the time when all basic city utilities were being created in The Dalles. Similar advances were being made in other towns directly adjacent to the Gorge, and would follow soon in most of the outlying areas. Telegraph poles and lines had been erected in earlier decades, running parallel to the river. Railroads followed the same general route on both the Washington and Oregon sides of the waterway. Electrical lines and poles were being added at the edge of town and sewer lines were constructed on a piece-meal basis as residents requested them and funding became available.

Community members tidied up and performed maintenance on a volunteer basis, but was it free labor with reimbursement for actual costs? At the city council meeting reported in the January 2 article of *the Chronicle,* the following bills were approved for payment:

Pacific Power & Light's horse-drawn pipe thawing outfit. Henry Rumsey in the cart and Frank John behind it. Electricity was drawn down from overhead lines through a wire, into the transformer on the wagon, then applied to the frozen pipe to thaw it. Courtesy of The Dalles Chronicle.

H. Glenn, mdse (merchandise) $2.15; M. T. Nolan, mdse $1.30; Dalles City Water Works, water for Dec. $50.00; F. S. Gunning, blacksmithing $5.15; H. Clough, repairs $2.00; Adolph Eglin, labor $1.00; Geo. Joles, labor $1.50; Seufert & Condon, telegraph $3.00; J. Like, hauling $.25; J. W. Blakeney, hauling $1.00; L. D. Oakes, hauling $1.00; Mrs. M. Hill, milk for Boffman boy $1.00; Hansen & Thompson, supplies $.45; Sexton & Walther, mdse $5.35; Columbia Hotel, meals to prisoners $1.50; J. P. Agidius, labor $37.60; Perry Van Camp, same $27.40; Lawson, same $19.40; J. Wettle, same $14.80; N. J. Love, same $19.60; G. H. Sparklin, same $7.20; Esther Nicholas, same $3.48; Margaret A. Martin, same 1.80; P. J. Martin, same $2.16; Kate McCormack, same $5.43; Matilda Baldwin, same $4.80; N. H. Gates, same $6.60; J. M. Marden, same $6.00; James Snipes, same $1.98; Z. F. Moody, for sewer pipe taken up $.75.

It appears repairs, updating, and progress made toward establishing sewer systems in that time frame were not yet being handled by city or county crews, although a local fire department had been officially established. The municipality certainly couldn't contract the jobs with crews from the growing metropolis of Portland, because there wasn't yet a cost-effective way to bring crews and equipment repeatedly to and from the east side of the Cascades. Again, transportation and distance were obstacles, but the pioneer spirit prevailed. If a skill set was missing in the community, somebody always managed to learn it when the time was right.

Residents themselves took on each task as time permitted them to do so, literally building communities of the Gorge brick by brick and board by board. In this way, the residents' tax dollars were returned individually when they performed certain community services. Local citizens invested in the success of their communities on a personal, as well as financial, level.

On the other hand, people didn't concern themselves much back then with being politically correct. Even newspaper articles tended to poke fun at community members and do a great deal of editorializing. The colorful language in this snippet from the October 6, 1902 issue of *the Chronicle* describes a mishap that occurred as a result of the changing times:

> This is nothing short of criminal carelessness to leave a gaping pitfall like the sewer ditches on a public highway without a danger signal, was proven by the accident which befell L.E. Crowe Saturday evening. Starting home from the store he proceeded to drive up Federal Street, for the moment forgetting the sewer ditch, when of a sudden his horse was precipitated into the ditch with the wheels on one side of the buggy in a like predicament, while he was thrown about ten feet on the debris ahead. Mr. Crowe was not seriously injured, the horse was somewhat cut and the buggy was badly demolished.

The October 6 issue also gives us a peek at some even sorrier circumstances the families had to endure:

> "At present there are five cases of diphtheria in the city—one at the Prinz', one at the Cosmopolitan [hotel] and three in a family by the name of Atkins camped in the pines. The latter is a very sad case, one child having died Saturday and the family is in destitute circumstances.

The urgency of area repairs and upgrades had diminished in comparison to all that had been accomplished during the previous several decades, but things were still moving along at a frighteningly rapid pace in the Gorge. In only five to seven decades, the first families in the Gorge needed to bring the standard of living close to the level enjoyed by people on the East Coast. Easterners had been building their infrastructure for 200 years. Even those in the Midwest had taken nearly 100 years to accomplish the same tasks.

Although Cascade Locks had opened downstream to provide greatly increased ease of access between The Dalles and the ocean during the previous decade, a problem remained just a short distance upriver: Celilo was not yet navigable. In 1906, plans were set in motion to build a Dalles-Celilo canal and the project was completed in 1915, connecting the lower and upper Columbia for virtually any watercraft.

As automobiles began to appear in communities along the Gorge, a whole host of new problems surfaced. Most roads were, at the time, merely paths created by wagons. Downtown streets were generally the only roads receiving regular maintenance and most of those weren't even graveled. At first the gas-powered vehicles were used only for short distances and on special occasions. It wasn't long before more were bumping their way over the wagon paths and their owners wanted to be able to drive greater distances from their own communities. They were ready to explore in the comfort of an automobile.

A vehicle could be brought by barge to any community that had a dock, but once it arrived where could it be driven? Neither the improved Barlow Road nor the more recent wagon road over the Cascades could be used for automobile travel. Something had to be done about roads on the Oregon side of the river. Great minds were already quietly working on the problem and the solution would have an enormous effect on the entire Gorge far into the future. But not yet.

The Mount Hood Railroad Company was formed on February 23, 1905, under the laws of the state of Utah, with legal headquarters in Ogden. It was promoted by a group of men associated with the Oregon Lumber Company, which had been operating near the mouth of the Hood River. As logging operations broadened, owners recognized the difficulties of driving large numbers of logs down such a turbulent stream. Noting the ever-increasing development of apple orchards on the east side of Hood River Valley, they determined it was time to develop a railroad to serve both lumber interests and the public at large.

Despite many delays, in March of 1906 the railroad was carrying supplies and materials bound for construction of the Oregon Lumber Company's new sawmill

November 5, 1896—the brand new "Regulator" dock, to take advantage of the first freight vessel to travel all the way from the sea to The Dalles. This dock would be the site of a major celebration commemorating the opening of the Cascade Locks. Courtesy of The Dalles Chronicle.

near the three forks of the Hood River. Materials were also being transported for the hotel to be built adjacent to the sawmill, to house its employees. Those two structures were the beginnings of the little town of Dee, named for Judge Thomas D. Dee, a vice president of the company who had died the previous year. A few years later the railroad expanded further, reaching its terminus at the location now known as Parkdale. The first regular train reached the Parkdale station on May 10, 1910. For a time, passengers and freight were loaded and unloaded at several stations and "whistle stops" along the route that were often named for the family that owned the adjacent land or built the depot or shelter at each location. With the increased use of automobiles for personal transportation and trucks for freight runs from the orchards to centralized packing facilities, use of the trains declined on this route. During interim years before all passenger service was discontinued in the 1930s, remaining passengers were served by a motorized coach affectionately known as the "Galloping Goose."

White Salmon, on the Washington side of the Columbia River, was experiencing a period of major growth as the twentieth century dawned. In fact, the entire north shore was experiencing a boom phase. Lying almost due north of Mount Hood and 50 miles south of Mount Adams, White Salmon sits atop a 600-foot steep basalt bluff and, for obvious reasons, boasts of one of the best views in the Pacific Northwest. From there one can see Mount Hood, a 25-mile stretch of the Columbia River, the entire Hood River Valley, and timbered hillsides. The view in summer is a spectacular contrast between Hood River's blooming orchards and a background of snow-capped Mount Hood.

Pioneers determined very early on that the Hood River Valley would be prime country for growing fruit. American Indians had long enjoyed an abundant crop of

One of the last Wasco County "horticultural fairs" held in Hood River, 1905. Hood River formed its own county shortly thereafter. The fair's theme was, "Ye Shall Know Them by Their Fruits." Courtesy of Hood River County Historical Museum.

volunteer strawberries, huckleberries, grapes, and many other fruits and berries prior to the arrival of the pioneers. The same was true on the Washington side at White Salmon, Bingen, and other little bergs nearby. The cultivated fruit crop here had grown to include pears, strawberries, apples, cherries, peaches, grapes, and tomatoes.

With annual rainfall in the valley averaging 30 inches, it wasn't necessary to irrigate the orchards. Because the rain fell gently rather than in torrential flows, even the most delicate cherry crop rarely suffered a loss due to a poor growing season. Winters on this end of the Gorge are mild and summers moderate. By the early twentieth century, the area was making a name for itself in the worldwide fruit market. Production in the Hood River Valley had grown exponentially in the 1880s and 1890s as the crop matured and orchards were planted when new settlers arrived. Local fruit growers on both sides of the river formed marketing cooperatives, allowing them to dominate the world markets for pears and apples beginning early that century.

The village of Trout Lake, Washington, had a busy dairy business going, shipping 1,800 pounds of cheese and 1,000 pounds of butter each week by 1903. On the north side of the Columbia, White Salmon and Bingen were bustling with activity. These two towns saw tremendous growth in the first decade of the new century for the same reasons Hood River's population had swelled during that time: excellent quality of life and a prolific fruit crop. The climate changes fairly rapidly between Hood River and The Dalles, permitting growth of oats and an excellent wheat crop in the drier eastern climate. If one were to combine all the resources of the area into a single meal, there would be a selection from beef, mutton, trout, or salmon as a main dish, potatoes and tomatoes or fresh biscuits with butter as a side dish, and a choice of fruits for dessert.

Rather than assess a tax on local residents, the custom of the day was to request "subscriptions" from local families and groups to support a capital project. This was the method used in 1896 to construct a landing to serve White Salmon and Bingen for boat traffic, at a cost of $2,000 plus subscription labor. The dock was deeded to The Dalles, Portland & Astoria Navigation Company in 1903 with the provision that the company maintain it. People landing at the new dock had a choice of walking a few hundred stairs up to the bluff or taking a horse-drawn carriage up the dock road to White Salmon. The stairway was set into the sidehill at an easy angle as part of the dock project.

A 1904 historical volume describes that "With the development of the district's strawberry industry during the latter part of the nineties, came a rapid settlement, creating a strong demand for a town upon the Washington shore." In the fall of 1901, A.H. Jewett purchased the old Cameron farm from the Ward brothers and platted the town of White Salmon. His first task, undertaken immediately, was to begin implementing a new water system. This system consisted of a Rife hydraulic pump capable of pumping ten gallons a minute 220 feet high, through a half mile of pipe. The water was supplied by a large spring located north of the church and distributed through a system of wooden and iron mains. A year later (1902) Frank Groshong opened a blacksmith shop. On May 8, 1903, the *White Salmon Enterprise* published its first issue, and shortly thereafter the Crow & Gearhart drugstore opened. By the end of 1903, several other businesses were operating in White Salmon, including:

Hyting Brothers, hotel; J.A. Fanning, men's furnishings; L.J. Wolfard, drugs; C.S. Bancroft, meat market; A.H. Jewett, brickyard (capacity 8,000 bricks per day); C.M. Wolfard, general store; M.C. Fox, confectionery; E.H. Dreske, jewelry store; Mrs. Jennie Green, dry goods and notions; Balsiger Brothers, general store; James Hancock, blacksmith; J.W. Eberhart, real estate; and Rosegrant & Eberhart, contractors. The town had both a doctor and a dentist: Dr. J.W. Gearhart and Dr. M.A. Jones, respectively.

Lodging facilities were added in 1904. J.W. Lauterbach began construction on a modern hotel at a cost exceeding $10,000. Two stage lines were running between White Salmon and several inland towns, including Camas Prairie, Glenwood; Trout Lake, Fulda, Gilmer, and Pine Flat.

For such a tiny community, the White Salmon–Bingen area made an impressive showing in the world fruit market early in the century. The local steamboat agent estimated the area was shipping 10,000 crates of strawberries, 10,000 cases of tomatoes, 5,000 boxes of apples, between 2,000 and 3,000 sacks of potatoes, and 1,000 boxes of peaches, along with large amounts of other products. Peaches, grapes, and cherries were (and still are) also raised in the area.

On the south side of the river, the Columbia Southern Railway had been completed to Shaniko in 1900, almost eliminating freight traffic over the Willamette Valley and Cascade Mountain Road/Santiam Pass. Not long after, on June 20, 1905, the first motor vehicle to cross the United States made its way over Santiam Pass to the Willamette Valley. Piloted by owner Dwight B. Huss, the Olds waited its turn at the toll gate while the gatekeeper tried to figure out what kind of toll he should charge for the noisy contraption belching smoke and snorting at him. Because the strange machine had scared horses and cows off the road and into the brush nearby, the gatekeeper deemed it a "roadhog" and charged a toll of 3¢—the rate for a pig.

Area sheep ranchers had been losing their herds to a condition known as scab, so in June of 1903 Wasco County Stock Inspector Dr. E.J. Young appointed three deputy stock inspectors to assist him in the south part of the county. The deputies would be G.W. Reeder, of Shaniko; Mr. Rooper, of Antelope district; and F.A. Young, of Young's district. The notice posted by Inspector Young in the *Chronicle* sternly warned that "any one found moving sheep without first being inspected or without passes, or any one knowing his sheep to be affected with scab, without giving me due notice, shall be fined to the fullest extent of the law."

As an annual gift to the community of its origins, Oregon Railway & Navigation Company (formerly Oregon Steam Navigation Company) offered an excursion rate to all Gorge residents who wished to travel during the summer of 1903 between The Dalles and Portland. Rates were $3 to make the round trip entirely on Sunday or $3.75 to depart The Dalles on either weekend day and return the following day.

Reflections of modern life also can be found during this first decade of the new century, as this cheeky snippet appearing in *The Dalles Chronicle* in March of 1903 presents a most interesting scenario:

> After the grist of marriage licenses which have been making their way into Hood River recently, it is only fair that the circuit court get in its work and furnish a divorce occasionally. The one applied for Saturday is somewhat out of the ordinary, the plaintiff, Joseph A. Knox, being 66 years of age and the defendant, Keturah Knox, 60. They were married on the 13th of May, 1900, after an acquaintance of one day, and the fair bride deserted her spouse three months later.

Area schools, of course, were still being heated with the abundant wood from local forests. According to a request for bids set forth by John Gavin, clerk of school district Number 12, the amounts to be used at each school in the 1905–1906 school year were as follows: 8 cords at East Hill Primary school, 20 cords at Court Street school, 24 cords at Academy Park school, and 80 cords at High school for a total of 132 cords.

An unprecedented five-day closure of all Oregon banks occurred November 1-5, 1907. Governor George Chamberlain issued the proclamation at the urging of a delegation of Portland bankers. Little notice was given, catching some local residents off guard and therefore financially handicapping them for five days. The reason was to avoid a run on the banks, similar to what would happen some years later, when the stock market crashed in 1929. Local bank patrons were understandably alarmed at such a drastic form of action, fearing their money was at risk. They were assured

Victor School, 1904. This was a classic country school. Classes were held only when the children were not needed in the fields for harvest or planting time, usually holding a two- or three-month winter session and a much shorter mid-summer session, six days a week.

by the two local banks, French & Company and First National Bank of Oregon, that the local economy was actually very healthy. Portland banks had advanced a great deal of money to people who weren't paying on their loans and thus approached financial instability. Local banks claimed they had no such problems, despite their custom of granting loans to farmers and ranchers in the off season, to be repaid immediately after each farmer's busy season.

Then there was the big cigar crunch of 1907. Cigar dealers said, "No more six for a quarter cigars." Some brands, it seems, were raising prices rather vigorously. Others were only seeing modest increases, but as J.E. Falt saw it, the retail pricing structure was due for change:

> We could not very well raise on those old-time brands at two for a quarter. If we were to charge a customer 30 cents for cigars he has for years been accustomed to buy for 25 cents he would get mad and we would lose his patronage. We must be ready to meet the advance in price in some other way.. It is most likely that the six for a quarter cigar proposition will have to be discontinued.

June 23, 1908, was a big day for the people who resided in the northwest slice of Wasco County in Oregon, for it became its own entity as Hood River County.

Hood River Sheriff Thomas Johnson watches over the catch-of-the-day on the Columbia River, 1918. Photo by LeRoy Childs, courtesy of Hood River County Historical Museum.

Very small in area by western standards, the county has only 533 square miles in which to conduct its business and is the second smallest county in Oregon. Majestic Mount Hood, named by its British discoverers in 1792 for Lord Samuel Hood of British admiralty, lies mostly within the county's boundaries. Sparsely populated at the time of formation, there were not enough financial resources available in Hood River to build a courthouse, so government services were provided from an old schoolhouse until 1937. At that time, still lacking resources to build a courthouse, the county bought the former Butler Bank building to house government offices until a new courthouse was finally built in 1954. This little county has made ingenious use of its natural resources during the past century, providing a year-round influx of money into the economy as a result. Agriculture, especially fruit, and hydroelectric production are mainstays, but Hood River county also relies on a year-round supply of recreational opportunities to fuel the economy.

At least one area resident attempted to improve his personal economy by divesting himself of a few family members. The *Chronicle* reported on January 5, 1909, that a chap by the name of Warren Kennedy who, five years and three children into his marriage to Mrs. Kennedy, refused to support the family further. A month earlier he had deposited his very pregnant wife and the two eldest children at a rooming house in The Dalles, and paid for a month's rent, light housekeeping, and a few days' worth of nurse services for after the baby's arrival.

He provided the family with a small store of food and promptly returned to his ranch about 8 miles outside of town.

We can only imagine the opinion most people had of Mr. Kennedy during the time when a new mother was expected to be bed-bound and tended to by a nurse for at least a few weeks after birth. Sheriff Levi Chrisman left no doubt about his opinion on the matter, arresting Kennedy and bringing him swiftly to trial. Kennedy was held on $500 bail, with the district attorney recommending the stiffest possible sentence of working for the county at $1.50 per day, with all proceeds going to Mrs. Kennedy, for "as long as Judge Lake sees fit to keep him at the job." The new baby was just two weeks old when Mr. Kennedy was taken to task by the Sheriff.

Across the river at White Salmon, acreages were selling like hotcakes. The corresponding desire for more cultural activities and entertainment pushed the opening of the Leo Theatre in 1912. Silent pictures were all the rage at the time, and resort properties and hotels were open for business. J.W. Lauterbach's Washington Hotel, finished in 1905, enjoyed about 10 years of prosperity, while the Jewett resort and one built by C.W.J. Reckers were both enormously popular, as vacationers could depart from the landing for a pleasant horse-drawn carriage ride out to the Guler Hotel in Trout Lake Valley if they wanted to get away. Most vacationers were the affluent of the Willamette Valley and their guests. Many United States dignitaries also had quiet vacations in the Gorge.

Moving back across the river to the Sherman County area in Oregon, the *Grass Valley Journal* reported a visit from Hector McDonald, who was buying horses for the English government for use in South Africa. The *Moro Observer* cited construction of the Moro Methodist Episcopal parsonage, the new Wasco Methodist Episcopal Church, the Wasco Opera House, plus a brick annex to the Moro School—all within the first decade of the century. The steamer *Columbia* was built at Rufus in 1902. Unfortunately, the *Columbia* ran aground very soon thereafter, and suffered severe damage. At least goose hunting was good, even when steamers weren't cooperative. Ben McCoy and Leon Moore bagged more than 50 of the birds while hunting just south of the Sherman County line (in Gilliam County).

In 1915, a seemingly small event quietly took place in the far western reaches of the Gorge. Portland lumber baron Simon Benson purchased 300 acres of land at Multnomah Falls and donated it to the city of Portland. As this plot of land was located adjacent to the planned Columbia River Highway, Portland opted to develop the area into a pleasant wayside stop for travelers, a park to provide "rest and refreshment." They had no idea Multnomah Falls was destined to become the most frequently-visited natural attraction in the state of Oregon.

Gorge residents have never been content to sit by and watch the world turn while they stood still. In November of 1887, Oregon voters defeated a proposed amendment to the state constitution to institute state-wide prohibition. In fact, saloons were allowed by law to operate in Oregon as the result of a measure approved by the voters in November 1889. The people had spoken, but the Temperance movement was gaining ground. On June 6, 1904, Oregon voters passed what was called a "local option" law. It allowed counties to implement liquor prohibition on a precinct-by-precinct basis. The law was approved by Legislative Assembly in 1905 and very soon after it was made official, the city of Hood River became the first town in the state to implement the practice of prohibition. Their desire for an alcohol-free zone may have come in part as a result of seeing what happened to nearby Cascade Locks (previously known as Whiskey Flat) in the 1890s.

Over the next decade, various Oregon counties and cities enacted prohibition via use of the local option. Before long, the state was again seriously considering a complete ban on liquor. The Women's Suffrage movement had hit Oregon in a big way to urge voting rights for women, and some of the suffragettes were also involved in the Temperance movement. Temperance gals felt the evils of the bottle were contributing to their lack of power in addition to being generally "wrong" for humankind. Women's Suffrage was enacted into law in 1912 in Oregon, so the only problem left for those women to conquer was the same bottle they had tried to quash (but without benefit of a vote) in 1887. On November 3, 1913, Oregon voters passed an amendment to the state constitution prohibiting the manufacture, sale, or advertisement of intoxicating liquor. In 1915, the Legislative Assembly enacted legislation implementing statewide prohibition, effective January 1, 1916. It was a full three years before ratification of the 18th Amendment to the Constitution paved the way for alcohol to be banned across the nation. They had voted to make Oregon a dry state. The following appeared in the January 6, 1919 issue of *The Dalles Chronicle*:

> Carrying a dress suit case which was suspiciously heavy and from which there emanated suspicious gurgles, Robert L. Boehmer, a discharged soldier, was arrested by Chief-of-Police Gibons last evening. Examination of the suit case showed that it contained a number of pint bottles of whiskey.
>
> When interrogated, Boehmer declared that he had secured the bottled goods in Portland and that he was taking it as a gift to friends in Sherman county. When arraigned before Police Judge Cates this morning, however, he pleaded guilty and was fined $50, which he paid.
>
> Papers which Boehmer carried showed that he enlisted at Prosser, Wash., and was assigned to service in the spruce division. He was given his discharge at Vancouver Barracks on December 18. He was still in uniform when arrested here.

Three days later, some sobering information appeared in an obituary-style article posted in the *Chronicle*. This was a matter of far greater importance to most people than their rights to enjoy happy hour. The killer influenza was raging in the Gorge and many residents had fallen ill with pneumonia often resulting from the flu. This obituary/article announced the deaths of two local females, Mrs. F.E. Cotty and Miss Mary Eslinger. Mrs. Cotty's only son was fighting in the war at the time of her death; Miss Eslinger had just turned 15 the previous November

26. The article reported 26 new cases of influenza documented by the health department the previous day and 30 the day before that, adding "the second crest of the epidemic remains about the same, 34 cases in a single day having been the maximum." With tuberculosis still alive and well, the impact of a killer flu was even more burdensome than it might have been at another time.

One loophole in the prohibition law was a provision for "personal medicinal use" liquor products. Stills sprang up in some of the strangest places, and of course they were not all for personal use and lawmen couldn't keep up with them. Most of the Gorge is flanked by the Cascade mountains, so it was certainly easy enough to hide a still—especially if one was willing to hide it some distance up the hillside. Nature was rife with camouflage that could be used to disguise a still. Rumrunning came into vogue and, unless a lawman wanted to try to follow the still owner up the mountain, he wasn't likely to find it. And if a fellow had registered his still for personal use, lawmen weren't likely to follow him at all as they could only cite someone if the still was considered to be too high capacity for personal use.

Like anywhere else, there were several bootleggers selling their "hooch" throughout the Gorge. But prohibition, or in some cases, the threat of it, sparked some creativity in western entrepreneurs. All sorts of new products were created in the 1890–1930 era, and some very clever advertising followed in the form of product names and labels. When an old boozer gave up the booze, the entrepreneur figured, he would be looking for other ways to spend his money—bottled non-alcoholic drinks. The state of Oregon registered hundreds of new trade names and labels as a result. One eastern Oregonian, however, became so disgruntled that he registered a trademark for "Nothing," which drew

Prohibition inspectors make a dockside find. Courtesy of Oregon State Archives.

some attention from the state. Jesse Day of Prineville's "Nothing" was registered in the product category of his choice: a Temperance Beverage.

The October 6, 1922 issue of the *Chronicle* carried a brief article about one of the local bootleggers who was busted. A raid had been conducted the previous day on the farm of H.L. Morse, 3 miles east of Friend. The raid yielded two 50-gallon kegs of prune mash, which were confiscated by Sheriff Levi Chrisman and Deputy G.L. Coleman. Only the sheriff and his deputy will ever know with certainty what happened to the 100 gallons of mash, but Morse pleaded guilty to charges of manufacturing and possessing illicit liquor. The fine was $250.

Finally, an initiative petition for some relief was filed with the state and the matter included on the November ballot in 1932. Voters chose to eliminate virtually all penalties from Oregon law relating to prohibition. They couldn't vote prohibition itself out, but they could eliminate the penalties. The entire nation was tired of prohibition by then, though, and in preparation for a repeal of the federal law, Oregon's voters repealed the state law in the summer of 1933. Shortly thereafter, Oregon ratified the 21st Amendment to the Constitution and federal prohibition was no more.

A cartoon that ran in Oregon newspapers right before the election outlawing liquor statewide in 1916. The message is clear. Courtesy of Oregon State Archives.

10. Making Connections and Entertaining Dignitaries

The Roaring Twenties were just that in the Gorge—roaring. The entire Gorge community was linking up, bridging, and doing anything else they could to connect their somewhat isolated towns to the rest of the Pacific Northwest.

One of the connections that had the greatest impact was the scenic Columbia River Highway, which would link the Gorge with Portland by automobile. The brainchild of visionary Samuel Hill and the engineering miracle of Samuel C. Lancaster, the highway created several firsts. It was the first modern highway constructed in this part of the Pacific Northwest, and the 74-mile stretch between Troutdale and The Dalles holds the honor of being the nation's first scenic highway. It is also one of the earliest examples of cliff-face road building using modern highway construction techniques in the United States. The project began in 1913 and was completed in 1922. The entire highway spanned the distance from Astoria at the mouth of the Columbia River to where the river turns northward west of Pendleton, but the scenic portion originates at Troutdale and terminates at The Dalles. From its inception it was proudly called "The King of Roads" by area residents.

Sam Hill envisioned a pleasant stretch of road that would blend into the natural beauty of the Gorge. Between the need to complement rather than disrupt the landscape, and the difficulty of building a highway into a basalt cliff, it was a pretty tall order to fill. His additional requirements for mild grades and the need to incorporate several bridges and other features into the highway made it a very specialized design job. Lancaster, an engineer and landscape architect, was noted for laying out Seattle's Lake Washington Boulevard. He and Hill had attended the first International Road Congress in 1908 and while there, toured western Europe to learn more about local roadbuilding techniques. Upon their return from Paris, Lancaster constructed experimental roads at Hill's Maryhill ranch on the Washington side of the Columbia, about 120 miles east of Portland. The combination of these experiments and what they had just seen in the Rhine River Valley in Europe inspired Hill to propose the scenic highway in the Gorge. It also was the inspiration for what eventually became Maryhill Museum, which is discussed later in this chapter.

Hill recommended Lancaster as the principal designer of the Columbia River Highway's scenic portion. Lancaster and the other designers on his team fastidiously held to a set of very strict standards for ease of driving, safety, and scenic considerations. Their design emulated European road-building techniques while maintaining complete respect for natural surroundings specific to the Columbia River Gorge. The road was to have no grade that exceeded five percent, a turn radius of 100 feet was calculated into every curve, reinforced concrete was used in every bridge, and matching masonry guard rails, guard walls, and retaining walls would be used throughout the project. Lancaster successfully created a stretch of highway that had natural beauty that blended into its surroundings without disrupting them.

Travelers were to be treated to breathtaking sights all along the highway, with convenient stops at sights like Multnomah, Bridal Veil, Horsetail, and Oneonta falls, as well as the Mosier Twin Tunnels and several other falls and viewpoints. The highway was immediately well-traveled, a showpiece of both form and function. In 1925, the lodge was built at Multnomah Falls, putting a final feather in the cap of the highway project. Portland architect A.E. Doyle designed the stone lodge structure and it was constructed by the Civilian Conservation Corps. at a cost of $75,000. The lodge remains in use today.

Between 1890 and 1919, the Hood River Valley growers enjoyed greater crops of better apples every passing year. The fruit had earned worldwide acclaim and the Hood River name was widely known, particularly for the Newton Apple. In 1919, the sky fell on local orchard owners when a disastrous freeze struck, killing a large number of apple trees. The next two winters were also harsh, and another Arctic-style frost hit the Gorge in 1921. Many of the smaller orchard owners sold their properties, unable to bear the repeated losses. The better-funded, larger orchards were replanted with pears, rather than apples. The result? The Hood River Valley became the world leader in pear production.

The year 1921 brought additional freedom to residents on the Washington side of the Gorge. The first road going directly to the Portland-Vancouver area was completed, shaving a significant amount of time off the trip as compared to the previous trail used. This stretch of highway is now known as Highway 14. Although not fully paved, it was considered far improved from the old road, which had taken a roundabout path and was positively full of chuckholes.

There was still a bit of "Wild West" left in the towns and cities of Oregon, and Gorge residents were not to be left out of anything. The October 20, 1921, edition of *The Dalles Chronicle* bore the headline, "Rail Officials Dance to Pistol Rag." The article follows:

> O. W. R. & N. Bosses Have Dull Evening Brightened; Shots Strike Car
> A special train arrived from Portland last night with railroad officials and was side tracked in the block east of the depot near the Umatilla house when the shooting began. A. Buckley, superintendent, and J.F. Corbett, assistant superintendent, were sitting on a baggage truck according to their story.
>
> When the bullets began to whiz in their direction, they decided it was time to hunt cover. Corbett is not a small man and Buckley will tip the scales

The effects of automation in the Gorge, looking east from Fifth Street to Oak Street in 1920. Highway Motor Company on left with a single gas pump on the sidewalk, dairy processing plant directly across the street, and Paris Fair and Bartmess Furniture retailers a bit further down on the right. Electrical transformers present on power poles. Photo courtesy of Hood River County Historical Museum.

at about 275 pounds. They tried hiding under the truck and behind telephone poles, which was not at all satisfactory, the telephone pole especially being too narrow for a man of Buckley's dimensions. He then ran for the depot.

Joe Hanley and John Murphy arrived on the scene from Hotel Dalles and immediately sought shelter under the special car. When the confusion had subsided, the railroad officials called for an engine and left the city. Their car was reported by spectators to have been perforated by shots.

A sub-heading and an additional article followed the first one, stating "Coast Tong War at Bottom of Trouble." It seems Officer Frank Heater and the railroad men were in the wrong place at the right time. But as further research by a modern-day *Chronicle* staffer indicates, Heater was also in exactly the right place. An inch or two in either direction might have been the end of him. One bullet struck him in the chest and lodged in his badge, proof that a little piece of metal really can save a life. He was treated for chest trauma and a bullet wound to his left leg.

Chinese workers had begun to trickle into Oregon as early as the 1850s, increasing in number when gold was discovered in the eastern part of the state in the 1860s. Over a period of time, a Chinese community formed in the Gorge and elsewhere in Oregon. The original United States home base for these people was

Mosier Trading Company, about 1890, one of the first businesses to take space downtown. Courtesy of Penny Kennedy.

in California, for they had immigrated when the Gold Rush began. According to the *Chronicle*, a tong war between different family groups was problematic across the entire West Coast. The Hop Sing-Suey Sing tong war was the one that fueled the fire that started the scuffle in The Dalles.

The Hop Sings lived in The Dalles. The Suey Sings were from Portland, as were some other Hop Sings. The Sueys were one-up on their rivals in terms of murdering each other, so the Hops were looking to even the score. However, the Hops residing in The Dalles were mortally afraid of the Sueys, fearing the Portland group might think them an easy target. They had been keeping a guard posted in the window of the local Chinese headquarters, the Kwong Chung Wo store at 216 East First Street. As the *Chronicle* put it, "This is the reason why the local Hops have their lookouts posted along First street. Any strange Chinaman who lands in The Dalles is given a close scrutiny, and if he looks suspicious the local Chinese tip off the police."

Somehow, in the lookout's excitement he apparently misidentified the railroad officials as Suey Sing tongmen, so he took aim. One might think this was not too surprising to local community members, but the truth is the Chinese had never caused any such ruckus in town previous to that occasion. All local Chinese residents had gotten along with one another beautifully. It was a simple case of mistaken identity—and a nervous trigger finger.

In addition to Officer Heater and the two railroad officials, one other man was caught in the crossfire on the street. His first name was not given, but his father was Dr. G.E. Sanders, a fruit orchard owner. The Sanders boy, a senior in high school, was shot in the hip (buttocks) and the bullet passed cleanly through his thigh without hitting the bone. Though not a serious injury, it probably ended his career as a football quarterback at The Dalles High School, and very likely injured his pride.

Unfortunately Fay On, 40, who appears to have been the lookout man who started the shooting, was not so lucky. His thigh bone was shattered according to Dr. Thompson Coberth, who tended his wounds at the scene. The situation could have escalated into something much worse had Sheriff Levi Chrisman not arrived when he did. A surprisingly angry crowd had gathered at the nearby Black and White restaurant at the sound of the emergency bell downtown. Armed and ready, when the crowd saw Officer Heater and the boy were wounded, they went a little crazy. The Sherriff did a bit of crowd control and appealed to their sense of order, asking them to show patience while he investigated the matter. Gunshot victims were taken to the hospital in private vehicles. Dr. Thompson Coberth treated Fay On's fracture. On April 20 the following year, the tong wars did indeed result in the death of a local member of the Hop Sing tong. Aged cannery worker Chang Hong was murdered by Chin Sic.

Meanwhile, one local chap was facing a serious dilemma. Suffering from severe arthritis, Ollie Lash could not plow and work his orchard in the Three Mile district near The Dalles. About 40 friends and neighbors did what they felt was the appropriate thing—they showed up at his home on April 28, 1922 with 10 teams of horses and equipment to work the Lash orchard. What's more, they brought their own coffee to keep everyone moving.

In June of the same year, the still relatively new Oregon Growers Cooperative was shipping Royal Anne cherries just about as fast as they could be picked. In the course of just 24 hours, they shipped out four railroad carloads of the succulent fruit. About the same time, a boxing match was held to entertain the local men. As the *Chronicle* so aptly stated, resident Ben Mullen "became so enthusiastic" that he climbed into the ring and "attempted to assist one of the fighters with liquid refreshment." He was arrested and charged with drunkenness.

Certain other rules were much more relaxed or didn't exist at all. Evidence of this came in February of 1923 when some chickens flew the coop, so to speak. Mr. and Mrs. A.M. Patison had recently moved to The Dalles from Wamic. Accustomed to country life, the Patisons let their chickens out "to range" one afternoon while they repaired the new chicken yard. It is hard to say exactly where the chickens found their new "rangelands," but they apparently found a patch of grass behind the sheriff's office or wherever law enforcement was dumping confiscated liquor products. They set off down the alley and didn't return until late that evening. Much to the Patisons' surprise, the chickens were thoroughly intoxicated when they returned to the chicken yard.

A mysterious item appeared in a late November 1922 issue of the *Mosier Bulletin*. A photo of a small group of Mosier residents appears with the caption saying a "mortgage burning" took place on November 25. Further research yielded no additional information. Was it an incredibly good year for crops, or were there some buy-outs made after the fact when the Columbia Gorge Highway was built? Perhaps the railroad bought a huge easement along the line?

In December 1924, another connection was made that would forever change life in the Columbia River Gorge. Less than two years after work began, Leslie Butler of Butler Bank drove the last spike home on the Waucoma bridge, which spanned the Columbia River at Hood River–White Salmon. Braving the chilly winter day, about 1,500 residents from both sides of the river crowded all the way to the center of the bridge in anticipation of taking their first walk to the other side. As a gift to the communities who had directly provided the initial funds for the project, builders would allow both foot and auto traffic to pass over the bridge without charge from the time of the dedication ceremony at 10 a.m. until 4 p.m. that day. People drove from as far away as Portland to be able to cross this landmark on opening day.

Beginning at 4 p.m., tolls were charged according to the following schedule: persons (walking), over 7 years of age, 10¢ (no charge under age 7, but no senior citizen discount offered); one person riding or walking with an animal, 50¢; bicycles, 20¢; motorcycles, 75¢; automobiles, 75¢; trucks, up to $5 depending on weight; and tractors, $5. An animal-drawn vehicle was charged 75¢ and up, depending on the number of animals providing power; a group of 10 or fewer animals were charged at a rate of 10¢ per head (plus the human companion), with a price break for more than 10 animals at 4¢ per head.

This bridge had been a dream of local residents for many years, but the idea was tabled as out-of-reach in the early 1920s when an engineer estimated such a bridge would cost about a million dollars. It was an impossible amount of money for this sparsely-populated area to raise, even with long-term financing options. Then one morning in 1923, engineers C.M. Chandler and Harry Gray changed everything by presenting plans for a bridge that could be built for considerably less than half of the previous estimate. Their proposal received the attention of many local residents, including Truman Butler of Butler Bank. Chandler and Gray explained how the majority of funds could even come from sources outside the immediate area, which made an immediate impression on Butler as his enthusiasm continued to grow. A group of local leaders was brought together to hear the proposal, and they concluded that there was no time like the present to build the bridge.

To prove the commitment of the local population to this monumental project, the group decided the best support would have to come in the form of cold, hard cash. Local residents would be required to contribute the first $70,000 to the bridge project (this number was later increased to $75,000). Using the usual subscription-based model, local businessmen set out to raise the "commitment funds." This would not be an easy task, as it was a difficult time for orchard owners and the local economy was generally depressed.

However, raise the money they did. Businessmen fanned out to target different areas; one group actually pitched a tent for four days on the Washington side of the river, asking for individual investments in $1,000 increments. Every $1,000 requested was roughly equivalent to asking for a $10,000 investment in today's dollars. The fund drive was surprisingly successful in a relatively short period of time, comfortably exceeding the required amount. Portland businessmen gave the bridge financing a significant shot in the arm by contributing an additional $100,000 (a million in today's dollars). The combination of the bridge and the new Columbia River Highway would make their investment well worthwhile by encouraging shoppers to travel to Portland and allowing easier shipment of mail-order goods.

Construction began in August 1923. Gilpin Construction Company was the contractor, with Professor C.B. Wind of Stanford University acting as consulting engineer. The bridge has 11 main piers, 30,000 feet of piling, 1.8 million pounds of fabricated steel, 5,000 yards of reinforced concrete, and 1 million board feet of lumber. The substructure was composed of steel and a 20-foot-wide plank roadway to top off the trusswork. The main bridge span was 2,134 feet, bringing the total bridge span to 3,700 feet including the timber approach ramps.

Designers were pleased to share the fact they were able to arrange the bridge at a height sufficient to avoid the need for a draw section at its center. One was quoted as saying, "By gaining height in construction, a draw is not necessary, and traffic will continue at all times." They did not envision the changes to take place the following decade, when the bridge had to be raised 27 feet to accommodate the reservoir behind Bonneville Dam. Even then, though, it was not necessary to have a draw bridge, and the cost of raising the bridge was borne by federal taxpayers. Other changes to the bridge over the years have included removal of the walkway to widen the driving surface, placement of a steel bridge deck, and realignment of the approaches. It was purchased by the Port of Hood River in 1950 at a cost of $800,000. An additional $725,000 was spent by the new owner during the following year for a major update.

This photo of the Eagle Creek Bridge demonstrates the elegance of the Columbia River Highway's construction. Masonry guardwalls and graceful curves are the hallmark of this scenic beauty. Cross and Dimmitt postcard image, contributed by Tony McLaughlin.

To gain a true appreciation of what a marvelous endeavor this new bridge was for locals, you only need to look at the numbers recorded by the Oregon-Washington Bridge Company for 1926: 22,114 pedestrians, 3,920 livestock, 67,432 autos, 67 stagecoaches, 1,778 motorcycles, 12,113 trucks, and 304 animal-assisted vehicles. By 1980, total bridge traffic had reached an astounding 1.2 million vehicles crossing over the Columbia River in just one year. Although locals do travel back and forth fairly frequently, much of this traffic is attributed to the many tourists who have discovered the essence of the Pacific Northwest. A family can easily spend its entire vacation exploring the Gorge, and many do just that.

1926 was a big year for residents throughout the Gorge. An international sensation was dedicated and officially opened to the public on November 3. The entire Gorge was abuzz, partly in anticipation of Maryhill Museum's holdings and partly because a queen was coming to do the dedication. No royalty had ever been through the Gorge before, much less stopped for any reason. Queen Marie of Rumania, her children (Prince and Princess Nicholas and Ileana respectively); French counselor Albert Thierman; Yakima Chief Alex Saluskin and his wife, Princess Klickitat; and Portland Mayor George Baker played important roles in the museum's dedication ceremony at the Maryhill Chateau. Many other important people from throughout the Pacific Northwest were among the thousands in attendance.

Railroad magnate and honorary Nez Perce Chief Samuel Hill envisioned Maryhill Museum as a world-class facility, which is exactly what it was from the very beginning and remains so today. Lying on the Washington side of the Columbia near the small town of Goldendale, seemingly miles from anyone or

Downtown The Dalles, looking east on Second Street. Many other businesses on this street have signs that can't easily be seen, but there should be no uncertainty about the direction to go to find the Walther-Williams garage. Courtesy of The Dalles Chronicle.

anything of real importance, the museum's location was no accident. It was chosen by Bruxelles of the Beaux Arts of France and the name by Jules Jusserand. Erecting the museum directly across the river from the highway on the Oregon side allowed travelers to see the perfectly manicured grounds and the chateau standing alone in the wilderness, an oasis near the river. The museum would be filled with select pieces of art, clustered in a thematic fashion according to their origins. Hill's international contacts had already evoked promised donations from multiple cultures before the museum's doors ever opened. Queen Marie's portrait would be hung upon the wall beside that of King Albert of Belgium.

After the dedication ceremony, Queen Marie was scheduled to depart with Hill at the wheel of a luxury car, then meet up with Oregon Governor Walter M. Pierce at Celilo. From there, her entourage would be driven to The Dalles for a short curbside reception in her honor, then on to Portland where she, her children, and attendants would depart on the long journey home.

The queen's anticipated arrival aroused such a stir in The Dalles that the crowd was worked up to a fevered pitch by the time she arrived. The street had been marked off to keep the general public at bay while public officials and social organizations made brief presentations. The queen's vehicle was to pull up next to City Attorney Celia Gavin's vehicle, allowing Miss Gavin to make a short speech and present her highness with a token of the city's affections. It would follow with a quick parade of women and girls from various social clubs and orchards, the ladies handing an appropriate gift to the queen as they passed by. Lavish gift baskets had been made up, full of fruits, canned salmon, and other delicacies from the Gorge just for this purpose. Alas, the crowd began to break through the barriers even before Miss Gavin had a chance to begin her speech, although she did manage a short greeting for the royalty. Gift baskets were quickly brought forward from behind the queen's car. With the crowd bearing down, ever closer to Queen Marie, Sam Hill put the car into gear, honked his horn and hastily pulled away from the crowd as the band played on.

In addition to the museum at Maryhill, Sam Hill had begun to construct a replica of Stonehenge that was finally completed in 1930. It was built as a memorial to Klickitat County soldiers who lost their lives in World War I. The inscription at the site reads:

> In memory of the soldiers of Klickitat County who gave their lives in
> defense of their country. This monument is erected in the hope that
> others inspired by the example of their valor and their heroism may
> share in that love of liberty and burn with that fire of patriotism which
> death can alone quench.
> James Henry Allyn, b. April 12, 1897; d. July 15, 1918
> Charles Auer, b. July 17, 1894; d. June 6, 1918
> John W. Cheshier, b. June 13, 1890; d. February 5, 1918
> Evan Childs, b. July 14, 1893; d. September 30, 1918
> Harry Cotfredson, b. May 6, 1894; d. July 30, 1918
> James D. Duncan, b. July 15, 1897; d. June 16, 1917

Robert F. Graham, b. February 29, 1896; d. April 17, 1917
Louis Leidl, b. March 5, 1894; d, October 14, 1918
Carl A. Lester, b. october 6, 1988; d. March 15, 1918
Edward Lindblad, b. March 25, 1899; d. September 15, 1918

Gorge residents have a reputation for showing their appreciation when it is appropriate to do so, and it doesn't stop at the practice of honoring people, as the next story will show. On December 19, 1928, the following article appeared in *The Dalles Chronicle*:

> Records showing that a Dalles dog, 'Tip" was officially discharged from the United States army, have been uncovered by employees of the adjutant-general's office at Salem during the reclassification of the old war documents. Tip was mustered out of service with Company L, Second Oregon infantry, with which Company G of The Dalles was merged at the Presidio, San Francisco, August 7, 1899. The dog had been with the army two years, and had been in 54 engagements, it was said.
>
> According to Fred Kennedy of The Dalles, who well remembers the animal, it was originally owned by Ben Ulrich who sold or gave Tip to Chris C. Lowe. Just how Tip happened to join Company G is not in the histories. The records show that the dog was enlisted for the duration of the Spanish-American war. At the time of its enlistment, it was 1 year, four months old; 1 foot 4 inches tall, fair complexion, brown eyes and white hair. Its occupation was given as that of a "bull pug".
>
> Under the heading of distinguished service appears this record: "Caught chickens for the company, which grub was scarce on the firing line. Tip participated in all the major insular engagements and skirmishes, taking part in the capture of Manila, the battle of Malabon and Polo and other campaigns. Mr. Kennedy vouches for the fact that Tip performed a real service in the procurement of chickens, the dog having helped the local veteran bring in 13 fowls in an evening. Other members of the Billy Fields post here remember Tip and are interested to learn that the dog's military service record was as carefully kept as that of the regular soldier."

On August 2, 1934, Eleanor Roosevelt, First Lady and wife of Franklin Delano Roosevelt, gave local residents a thrill as she passed through The Dalles on her way to meet her husband in Portland. President Roosevelt was scheduled to arrive the following day aboard the cruiser *Houston*. Such mingling would be unheard of just 30 years later. The First Lady even drove her own car! Stopping briefly at the edge of town to receive a bouquet of flowers and a hospitality letter from the city, she even declined the offer of Police Chief Frank Heater to provide her with an escort.

Officer Cliff Allen made the presentation to Mrs. Roosevelt, having been sent by Celia Gavin, city attorney and the commissioned representative of the local branch of Daughters of the American Revolution. Informed of her impending arrival ahead of time, the *Chronicle* stated, "Business men, acting spontaneously, had placed flags for the length of Second street as reports were current during the morning that she planned to pass through here after leaving Bend, where she spent the night."

The First Lady smiled and waved at the crowds the entire time while following an Oregon State Trooper quickly through the main business district of town. He seemed to relish the honor, announcing Mrs. Roosevelt's appearance with intermittent taps of his car horn the entire distance.

World War I soldiers and Red Cross workers pose together for this photo with community members. Most likely taken at time of the swearing-in ceremony in The Dalles. Courtesy of Barbara Cole.

11. Columbia Rolls On Until Miss Helen Blows Her Top

President Roosevelt himself was quite familiar with the Columbia River Gorge. Prior to signing the 1937 act authorizing Bonneville Power Administration (BPA) to operate Bonneville Dam, the President personally visited the area, staying in a local hotel but otherwise keeping a fairly low profile. BPA, the principal energy wholesaler in the Pacific Northwest, manages the power generation and distribution of several dams in the region. Bonneville Dam construction was authorized in 1930 and commenced in 1933, and the dam was fully operational by early 1938. It was the first dam to be built in the Columbia River Gorge, followed by The Dalles Dam (1960) and John Day Dam (1971). While crop irrigation has been significantly enhanced, boats of all sizes can navigate the river for hundreds of miles and electricity there is some of the least expensive to be found anywhere in the nation. However, the dams have caused more controversy in these parts than just about anything else in history.

Things started out well. The federal government's now-infamous "308 Report" provided recommendations for "improved water infrastructure" along the Columbia River. After Grand Coulee Dam was completed for flood control, the report turned its attention to the proposed site of the Bonneville Dam. Area farmers were most interested in the irrigation possibilities on the horizon if a dam was built on the lower Columbia, but they were experts on the subject of upsetting the balance of nature. Many local citizens were just excited about the potential for lower electricity bills. Their current power generation facilities left much to be desired, but would a dam on the Columbia really be the answer to their problems?

When the idea was "sold" to them, it sounded enticing: even river navigation would become easier due to the navigation locks that would be built into the dam. And the project would employ many local workers, not to mention pumping a large amount of money into the community in other ways. Since most residents had virtually no knowledge of or experience with the requirements and implications of a massive hydroelectric project, not many hard questions were asked. One segment of the local population, however, was visibly upset about the project, and they voiced their concerns. Members of Native American tribes who had fought hard to retain their valuable salmon fishery were more than a little bit concerned, and rightfully so.

Water levels behind the first dam would be increased by about 27 feet, effectively flooding every fishing platform and every fishing hole east to Hood River that had been used for centuries by the Indians. Salmon was the single most important resource the tribes had. By flooding the rapids behind the dam, the government would deprive the Indians of part of their established salmon fishery. The tribes were assured that they would still be able to fish in the Columbia. Fish ladders would also be installed to allow the fish to safely navigate upstream each year to their spawning grounds

One big problem created by the second dam was that Memaloose Island (literally "Island of the Dead" in Chinook trade jargon), a sacred, ancient Indian burial ground, would be submerged. There was but one solution to the problem, since the government was determined to have its dam. The ancient remains were unearthed as much as possible prior to allowing the reservoir to fill, and reburied nearby. The most visible loss of all, though, was Celilo Falls. This historic fishery was completely destroyed in 1957, although every effort was made to preserve the ancient petroglyphs and other items of historic and archaeological significance to the cultural trade center at the falls. The loss of the historic fishing grounds is still mourned by local tribes.

Once the first dam was built, BPA needed to do some public relations work to encourage people to view dams as positive things. Their PR campaign included

Some of the fishing platforms next to the falls, along with one of the cross-river tram bases constructed to move people and supplies back and forth in cable cars. Courtesy of The Dalles Chronicle.

creating two movies, as well as numerous public service announcements for radio. They also paid Woody Guthrie to write some songs about the river and the dam. He moved to the area briefly in 1941 so he could receive inspiration from the Columbia River itself, churning out a total of 26 songs and creating several radio spots in one month's time. One of those tunes, "Roll On, Columbia, Roll On," was played on the radio for many years after. This was apparently a donation on Guthrie's part, as at least one source says he was paid just $266 for his efforts. From "Roll on Columbia, Roll On":

> Roll on, Columbia, roll on.
> Your power is turning our darkness to dawn,
> So, Roll on,
> Columbia, roll on!
>
> At Bonneville now there are ships in the locks,
> The waters have risen and cleared all the rocks,
> Ship loads of plenty will steam past the docks,
> So, Roll on, Columbia, Roll on!

The manmade Bridge of the Gods spans the Columbia River at the approximate location of the legendary natural bridge near Cascade Locks, a short

A bare stretch of the Columbia River Scenic Highway immediately after it was completed. Cross and Dimmitt postcard image, contributed by Tony McLaughlin.

distance upriver from Bonneville Dam. In fact, the northern pilings are secured in remnants of the natural bridge. Many of the boulders that made up part of the once-dreaded rapids on the Columbia were blasted into much smaller pieces with dynamite when the new dam and locks were constructed. Although most of the river's original features were lost to the rising waters, the stone masonry of the old canal at Cascade Locks can still be seen.

The real war—World War II—began on December 7, 1941. The following day's newspaper contained an anti-hysteria message, assuring residents that there was no need to panic in expectation of being bombed. The same day, The Dalles City Council met with other local officials, members of the county defense council, and other public groups. The sheriff also said local "Japanese citizens, through Harry Morioka, have volunteered their services in any way that local officers may see fit to use them." Sadly, those same Japanese citizens were later forced by federal order to go live in the Japanese "camps" until the war was over.

World War II brought with it many new and unusual national mandates, such as rationing and recycling. Gorge residents were up to the challenge and more than willing to do whatever they could to support their troops. The following war-related announcement, printed in the June 30, 1942 *Chronicle*, was typical of the periodic updates issued during that war:

> Following hard on the heels of President Roosevelt's announcement that the national drive for scrap rubber will be continued for an additional 10 days, Ole Larson, general chairman of the Wasco County campaign, reported this morning that all company operated service stations in this area will be closed between the hours of 12 and 6 p.m. All independent stations are also being requested by the Mid-Columbia oil companies to close their doors during the same hours and thus allow their employees to devote the time to scouring the respective areas for more rubber. Announcement that rationing stamps Nos. 5 and 6 each are good for two pounds of sugar was received by the local rationing board from the Office of Price Administration. Stamp No. 5 is valid from June 28 to July 25. Stamp No. 6 is valid from July 26 to August 22. The change in regulations does not increase the amount of sugar allotted to each consumer but has been put into effect to do away with the use of so many stamps, it was pointed out by Mrs. Helen Knight, office manager for the Wasco County board.

Although local resident Rodger Nichols was born more than a decade after the war broke out, he offered an interesting story that has largely been forgotten by the few area residents who ever knew it. Currently copy editor at *The Dalles Chronicle*, he was employed at radio station KODL in The Dalles for a number of years prior to taking his newspaper post. A former KODL station manager told Nichols a small cottage was built behind the radio station during the early days of Word War II, when the Japanese were sweeping through the South Pacific, seizing islands. There

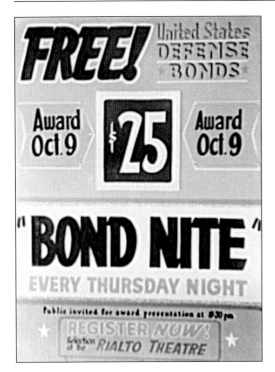

The local movie theatre offered "Bond Night" every Thursday night in support of the war effort. Library of Congress photo.

was great concern that the Japanese would attack the mainland, finding targets for their bombers by using radio station signals as direction finders. Nichols explained:

> So every morning before West Coast stations as far inland as The Dalles were allowed to sign on, they had to wait for an all-clear signal . . . that signal was given only after shore-based planes flew out to sea and checked to be sure there were no Japanese carrier groups lurking just over the horizon, preparing to launch. The hut was built so that a station employee could sleep there overnight, with an alarm rigged up to the teletype to wake him up in case there was a need to sign the station on and warn the civilian population.

With well over 2,000 of the Gorge's finest men in military uniform during the war, every community had a vested interest in it, and each took its role very seriously. For modern evidence of their commitment, we have only to recall how many of our parents or grandparents continued to save aluminum foil long after the war was over, meticulously flattening and smoothing it for later use.

However, not everything that happened in the 1940s was related to the war. One interesting item found in the 1942 newspaper archives was an article about workmen beginning the process of removing debris and salvaging items after the "recent fire" at the Horn Saloon in The Dalles. The article is dated May 6, 1942, but no additional information is known about the fire that apparently occurred in either April or May. No mention is made of the saloon's owners, but the article does say, "while definite plans have not yet been announced, it is understood that the building will be reconstructed, eliminating the second story, providing priority ratings can be obtained for essential materials." The Horn Saloon was originally owned by Charles Frank until his death in 1906.

A gas mask was passed around at the July, 1942 City Council meeting in The Dalles, to familiarize city officials and others present with the way the apparatus worked. Fire Chief Charles A. Roth, Jr., the designated defense counsel gas mask training instructor, had received 62 masks the day before, which were to be distributed to appropriate organizations. Roth distributed 18 masks to the Oregon Women's Ambulance Corps., 15 each to the police department and fire department, 14 to air raid wardens, and 8 to W.L Kirk's rescue squad. The Red Cross held a fund drive in March 1943 as the war progressed and intensified. The Wasco–Sherman County chapter was led in the fund drive by Mrs. L.L. Hickok.

Finally, the rationing and the war both ground to a halt. On September 1, 1945, the following article appeared in *The Dalles Chronicle*:

> The Dalles this week-end will enjoy the first two-day holiday since gasoline rationing was ended. As a result, numerous local residents are planning motor trips to various parts of the state, and many persons from other communities are expected here for visits. With the exception of a few service establishments, all stores and public offices in The Dalles will be closed all day Monday. The *Chronicle* will not be published, The postoffice will make no deliveries, but mail will be distributed to box holders.

It would be interesting to learn what kind of weather the rest of the world was having the winter of 1948–1949. January of that season was so cold, it reminded a few of the local oldtimers of the horrible blizzard that struck the Midwest in 1888. Interestingly, the coldest day in the Gorge in 1949 occurred exactly 61 years to the day after the big blizzard, on January 12. An unusually long period of sustained cold, with a low of 7 degrees, had paralyzed the region—nothing even close to the -32 degree temperatures and blowing snow H.G. Miller experienced as a lad of 11 years in Dustin, Nebraska—but debilitating to the local marine-based economy nonetheless. Most of the Pacific Northwest was similarly affected, some places were even colder, but the lower Columbia was freezing solid much more quickly than anyone had anticipated, which was a real problem. The January 12, 1949 issue of the *Chronicle* included an article about the predicament created by this cold snap. Power output was severely reduced at the dams, freight transport existed in a state of suspended animation, and even airmail deliveries were thrown off kilter:

> Ice completely blocked the Columbia river channel from Big Eddy to Crates Point west of The Dalles late yesterday, ending all navigation in

this area and hampering travel between the city and the airport. With The Dalles ferry icebound, the nearest river crossing is the Hood River Bridge. Floe ice, crunching as it moved, filled the channel yesterday and froze together, leaving the surface smooth as compared to conditions during similar cold spells in previous years. The first signs of buckling, however, were reported from the Big Eddy area, late this forenoon. If continued, this process could result in huge ice jams, the latest of which occurred in the winter of 1943.

The article explained that all Pacific Northwest dams were processing drastically reduced volumes, which of course resulted in an immediate reduction in hydroelectric generating capacity. In plain language, a dam can't generate power if water doesn't pass through the turbines. At that point they were producing less than half the usual amount of electricity during a period of increased consumption. Addressing the freight issue, the article said an Inland Navigation boat was icebound at Bonneville and the Winquatt tug was also biding time downstream with its five barges in tow.

The Columbia River eventually thawed out, of course, and things returned to normal. Normal, during this era, included yet another war. The Korean War came so quickly on the heels of World War II that many veterans were still in post-enlistment reserve status. So, along with a new crop of recruits from the Columbia Gorge and elsewhere, many of the veterans went right back in to fight again when the Korean War began in June 1950.

To those who lived almost anywhere else in the country, it must be unfathomable that the communities of the Gorge were affected so little by the tumultuous times of the 1960s and 1970s. The Gorge had been grappling with racism and equal rights almost since the moment the white man first stepped on the Columbia's shores, so there were no major scores to settle when the rest of the nation tackled those issues. Over a very long period of time, Native Americans had gone from being viewed as "redskins" and "savages" to having their culture appreciated and even celebrated by the rest of the local population. The real reason for the transition may have been because so many current residents descend from both European and Native American or Hispanic blood lines. The area has a large population of all three original bloodlines and, by default, the community as a whole is accepting of diversity. Not particularly quick to welcome it, but accepting.

Without Civil Rights conflicts and women's movement demonstrations, then, what exactly took place along the Columbia River during the 1960s and 1970s? The answer is "not much outside of the ordinary." Life went on in much the same way it always had before, with gradual shifts in the community as a whole. "Jesus People," halfway houses, and young people touting free love found their way to the Gorge. They were all generally accepted with a raised eyebrow here and a grin there, but nobody gave a lot of thought to them unless they caused trouble—which they generally didn't. The Gorge was too close to Portland to have been unaware of the changes taking place throughout the country, but it was

Downtown The Dalles, 1950, on a snowy winter's day. Courtesy of Barbara Coles.

separated by geography in a way that allowed Gorge dwellers to pay only as much attention to outside events as they wished to notice.

Regarding the Vietnam conflict in particular, resident Rodger Nichols summarized the situation this way:

> The Gorge, particularly that far back, was fairly conservative in general makeup. Disagreements were more likely to take place around a kitchen table than in the streets. Kids home from college, having plugged into the wider world and keenly aware of their chance to be forcibly sent to southeast Asia via the draft, clashed over the necessity to defend freedom on somebody else's turf with parents who were World War II vets. The parents' only experience was with a time when it was obviously necessary to do just that. There was a very real danger, had things tipped just a little too far the other way, of Japanese landing craft storming the beaches at Newport. While we were aware of that, we scoffed at the ability or desire of the Viet Cong to come charging over the Cascades.

Although perhaps it should have drawn more notice on a national level, Oregon's groundbreaking "bottle bill" went into effect in 1971. Even Oregonians didn't realize how far-reaching their little ecologically-correct bill would be. Governor Tom McCall, the bill's main proponent, may have been the only person with any inkling that within just a few years, the entire nation would be following suit in one way or another. McCall was known for his environment-friendly projects, as well as his openly anti-Californian attitude. Oregonians generally approved of his driving desire to keep Oregon clean, while often bristling at the tactics he used to accomplish that goal. His presentation of the bottle bill was well-timed and expertly executed, resulting in majority support for a change of monumental proportions.

The bottle bill was simple from the state's standpoint, but it completely changed the way bottling companies would do business in the future. To encourage recycling of glass bottles and aluminum cans, the bill proposed two major changes to the way pop and beer were packaged and sold to Oregonians. First, a refundable 5¢ deposit would be paid at the time of purchase: If the empties were returned to any store carrying that brand, the deposit would be refunded. The empties were hauled away from the grocery stores for recycling. Manufacturers were also required to design a can whose tab remained attached after the beverage was opened. Since Oregon was the only state with those requirements, manufacturers opted to change all of their factories to comply with Oregon's laws, rather than trying to tool their machines for two different kinds of cans.

Oregon's highways showed an almost immediate difference when the bill went into effect. Far fewer people chose to throw their empties out the car window and there were no more can tabs reflecting the sun along the roads. Other states took notice of the program's overwhelming success, but only a few have been willing to implement the entire program due to the burdens it places

Rowena Loops on the scenic highway offer an impressive view of the river, as well as of upcoming cliffs for those traveling east to west. Although guardrails meeting modern standards have been installed in recent years, it is still a road to drive slowly and enjoy the view. Contributed by Toni McLaughlin.

on grocery stores. Recycling programs now exist throughout the country and have grown into major enterprises as the nation has recognized their benefits. The popularity of Oregon's bottle bill remains high more than 30 years after its implementation and recycling has become a way of life for a large portion of the national population.

On November 24, 1971, the Pacific Northwest grabbed nationwide headlines. Dan Cooper, mistakenly called D.B. Cooper, hopped a Thanksgiving eve flight on Northwest Airlines from Portland to Seattle. A short time after departure he handed the flight attendant a note demanding $20,000 in cash and four parachutes, to be supplied at Seattle's Sea-Tac Airport. All passengers and most of the crew were allowed to deplane in Seattle. Once outfitted with his requested items, he wanted to be flown to Mexico. Specific instructions were given to the pilot: do not exceed 10,000 feet in altitude, have the landing gear down, and set the flaps at 15 degrees.

The only non-cockpit staff on the plane was a flight attendant, from whom Cooper received instructions on the exact mechanism used to open the back door. She was sent to the cockpit then and told not to return to the cabin until they made a refueling stop in Reno, Nevada. When the flight attendant went forward and turned to close the first-class curtain behind her, she saw Cooper putting something that looked like a cord around his waist. About 25 minutes into the flight, the pilot saw the indicator light blink on, notifying him the back door was open. A few minutes later, he asked through the intercom if Cooper needed anything more. Cooper's quick "No!" was the last they heard from him.

The para-jacker had clearly done his homework and there was every indication he meant no harm to airline personnel. He left two parachutes intact near his seat and a third packed chute was only missing its outer rope, which was probably what he used to tie the bag full of $20 bills to his waist. Leaving the gear down and flaps at 15 degrees created enough drag to keep the aircraft flying at less than 200 m.p.h., allowing Cooper to jump from the rear steps of the plane in flight. He had chosen the only aircraft with a rear staircase in a door under the tail. By making the pilot fly low and at slow speeds, Cooper not only made his own escape possible, but also preserved the lives of the crew. At higher altitudes they would have all been killed with the sudden depressurization of the aircraft.

It was originally thought that Cooper left the airplane slightly north of Vancouver, Washington. Information provided by the pilot several years later led some investigators to believe they may have focused their ground sweep too far west. On February 10, 1980, $5,800 in tattered $20 bills and several rubber bands were found by an eight-year-old boy digging a firepit along the north bank of the Columbia River just west of Vancouver. The serial numbers matched those included in the money given to Cooper and the rubber bands were of the same type used to bundle the money that day in 1971.

Despite countless hours of investigation by the FBI and several individuals, no other trace of Cooper has ever been found. Daniel Cooper faded into the Pacific Northwest somewhere, most likely between Vancouver and White Salmon, perhaps slightly north of the Columbia. The money found may have washed down one of the Columbia's tributaries and the rest could easily have been carried out to sea by the river. Was it the perfect crime or is his skeleton yet to be found? Either way, Cooper's para-jacking remains the only unsolved skyjacking case in federal aviation history. The case remains open.

The eruption of Mount St. Helens just three months after Cooper's stolen money was discovered, erased any chance of finding his remains or additional cash within the wide area destroyed by the eruption. Although debris from the eruption primarily traveled north of the mountain and Cooper is thought to have jumped south of it, the massive ash plumes left significant ash coverage hundreds of miles away.

Mount St. Helens, about 50 miles north of Hood River and White Salmon, had been rumbling and puffing smoke for a considerable period of time before its 1980 eruption. Its last had occurred in 1857. It was anybody's guess when or if she would actually blow. Serious seismic activity began on March 15, 1980, with more than 100 minor quakes recorded during the next seven days. The 4.1 tremor on March 20 caused minor snow avalanches in several locations on the mountain and convinced seismologists that Mount St. Helens would indeed erupt. As the number of earthquakes increased dramatically in the days following the first 4.1 disturbance, they installed several new instruments that would be used to pinpoint specific areas of activity under and around the volcano. Magnitudes of 4.0 or greater on the Richter Scale are classified by seismologists as significant quakes, particularly in relationship to a volcano that is threatening to erupt.

March 22 and 23 each brought one quake larger than a 4.0; the 24th brought four of this size and the 25th brought an astounding 25 tremors exceeding 4.0, 22 of them coming within a single eight-hour period. The Spirit Lake visitors' center was shut down and all forest service roads leading to Mount St. Helens were closed for safety. When the daily numbers of quakes could be measured in hundreds between March 25 and 27, they knew something was going to happen soon. They didn't have long to wait.

The first sighted explosion occurred on March 27. At 11:20 a.m., an Army National Guard reconnaissance flight reported seeing a hole in the icecap at the summit of the mountain and a grey streak extending southeast from the hole. At 12:30 p.m., a group of people near the mountain reported hearing a loud "boom." Shortly after, a Portland radio reporter saw "ash and smoke spewing out, a little like smoke out of a chimney" when he flew over. At 2 p.m., seismologists recorded a 4.7 quake followed by a black plume rising to about 7,000 feet above the volcano. A 200- to 250-foot wide crater formed in a fat crescent shape following the explosion.

Nearby residents who remained within a 15-mile radius of the volcano were urged to pack their belongings for a quick departure. Local law enforcement evacuated additional people on the north fork of the Toutle River, as well as diehard scientists and reporters at Spirit Lake. As is always the case with evacuations, some people wanted to stay until the last possible moment and others had no intention of leaving at all. Scientists were reasonably sure a full eruption would not bring a lava flow but they predicted mud slides, flooding, and suffocating ash. Even they weren't fully prepared for the volume of either ash or mudslides Miss Helen would serve up. The following day brought a dozen or more rounds of rumbling and belching, throwing even larger plumes of steam and ash much farther than the first day. The day's ash-belching events (scientists call them phreatic explosions) distributed enough ash particulate into the air to trigger a fatal asthma attack for the author's sister-in-law, Delora Higginbotham Dohnal, nearly 100 miles away in Pasco, Washington.

Long-time Spirit Lake resident Harry Truman steadfastly refused to evacuate. A *Longview Daily News* article quoted Harry as saying, "I think the whole damn thing is overexaggerated . . . Spirit Lake and Mount St. Helens are my life . . . You couldn't pull me out with a mule team." Harry and his St. Helens Lodge became a legend in their own time as the big bang drew nearer in the weeks that followed. The mountain was his home and he had planned for some time to eventually die there. As he put it, "I've lived here over 50 years . . . That mountain's part of Harry and Harry's a part of that mountain."

Volcanic activity of all types increased exponentially over the next few days and a second crater formed. A total of 93 explosions occurred on March 30. The two craters grew toward each other until they formed a single massive crater about 600 feet wide. A deformation became noticeable on the north slope. Hundreds of people poured into the areas immediately outside the road blocks, wanting to see history in the making. Ash was reported in noticeable quantities in the Bull Run Watershed on Mount Hood, and Cowlitz County, Washington, declared a state of emergency in hopes of getting National Guard troops to assist with evacuations and roadblocks. By mid-April, seismic activity became less frequent and decreased in intensity. The crater was still belching ash as high as 20,000 feet and the expanding chasm had widened to about 1,500 feet by April 3. Four days later it had widened about 200 feet, to measure 1,700 by 1,200 by 500 feet deep.

The calm before and after the storm: Mount St. Helens as seen from the ridge occupied by David Johnston the day before she erupted, and again four months after. The blast lowered the summit of the mountain more than 1,300 feet. USGS Photos by Harry Glicken, May 17 and September 10, 1980.

Washington Governor Dixie Lee Ray declared a state of emergency throughout the state and appropriate emergency information brochures were composed. Ash was traveling great distances already, and the governor expected that the worst was yet to come. Roadblocks proved fruitless in nearby Cowlitz County (Longview area). So many people were coming to see the volcano that the state highways were bumper-to-bumper along the roadside, all the way to the roadblock. If an evacuation had needed to be made quickly, it would have been impossible to execute. Aerial photos taken by the United States Geological Survey (USGS) on April 7 were converted to topographical maps and compared to photos taken using the same parameters prior to the March activity. The maps were available for use on April 23, at which time scientists were able to measure the changes. Parts of the north flank, where a bulging "irregularity" had become much more obvious, had actually expanded outward 300 feet in a matter of weeks.

Outward signs of an impending eruption became less visible in the next few weeks. The bulge continued to grow at a rate of about 5 feet per day and seismic activity remained as intense as it had been, but without considerable displays of puffing smoke or awesome noises. The "newness" wore off in the eyes of many outside the scientific community and it became increasingly difficult for the

May 18, 1980—Smoke, ash, steam and rock are blown skyward as Mount St. Helens begins her full-fledged eruption. USGS Photo by Austin Post, May 18, 1980. All eruption details courtesy of USGS/ Cascades Volcano Observatory

scientists to convince the public that there would be plenty more to come. Logging operations had even continued nearby. The USGS surmised that one of the reasons people had not seen cause for alarm was their familiarity with the famous Hawaiian volcanoes and their slow-moving fluid lava flows—quite a different situation than the explosive dome building in the Northwest. One logger whose operations were focused just 10 miles from the peak of the volcano was quoted as saying, "I don't see any hazard. I just came back from Hawaii, where they run tourist buses right up to the edge of a venting volcano."

May 7 brought an end to the apparent quiet when plumes of steam and ash once again became visible on the horizon. Between March 20 and this date, a total of some 2,550 earthquakes had occurred exceeding 3.0 on the Richter scale, with 291 of those in excess of 4.0. A week later, explosions again ceased, although the bulge on the north flank continued its phenomenal rate of growth. Three workers were flown in on May 15 to retrieve equipment from the Boy Scout and YMCA camps on Spirit Lake. A group of property owners had increased pressure on local government to allow them back in to retrieve their possessions in the Spirit Lake area; on May 17 they signed waivers and were escorted in to the area by authorities. A second retrieval trip was scheduled for the following morning.

Finally, at 8:32 a.m. Pacific Daylight Time on the morning of May 18, 1980, an earthquake rattled the mountain measuring 5.1 on the Richter scale approximately 1 mile below the surface. This seismic activity would set events in motion. With such a shallow point of origin, the quake's jolt had nowhere to go but straight up and into the volcano. The quake threw large rocks into the puffing crater, and a massive chunk of the north face broke off the mountain. This first chunk of mountainside followed gravity down to the next section, picking up speed as the gathering landslide raced down the remainder of the north flank at a velocity of up to 150 mph. When all was said and done, the avalanche debris had a total volume of 23 square miles. It buried the north fork of the Toutle River to an average depth of 150 feet.

The lateral blast covered 230 square miles and reached 17 miles northwest of the crater, with a volume 250 million cubic yards. Depth of deposits from the explosion ranged from about 3 feet at the volcano's base to less than an inch at the edge of the blast. This powerful eruption reached a velocity of at least 300 mph with temperatures as high as 660 degrees fahrenheit, releasing 24 megatons of thermal energy (7 by blast and 17 through release of heat). Four billion board feet of timber (enough to build about 300,000 two-bedroom homes) were destroyed.

Prior to the eruption, Mount St. Helens's summit height was 9,677 feet; its post-eruption level was 8,363 feet high; a total of 1,314 feet was removed as a result of the event. Crater dimensions immediately prior to eruption were 1.2 miles east-to-west, 1.8 miles north-to-south, and 2,084 feet deep with a crater floor of 6,279 feet.

Effects of the eruption were immediately visible but it took months to fully assess the damages. The ash plume reached about 80,000 feet in less than 15 minutes and spread across the country in just three days, circling the Earth in 15 days. The total volume of ash to leave the volcano was 1.4 billion cubic yards; detectable amounts covered 22,000 square miles. Ash and pumice accumulated to 10 inches deep at 10 miles downwind, 1 inch deep 60 miles downwind, and 1/2 inch deep 300 miles downwind—effectively blanketing the states of Washington and Oregon with 1/2 to 10 inches of abrasive ash. Varying amounts hung in the air constantly for several weeks after the eruption.

Lahars, commonly known as volcanic mudflow, damaged 27 bridges and nearly 200 homes. More than 185 miles of highways and roads and 15 miles of railways were also destroyed. Mudslides that filled tributaries fed so much debris into the Columbia that its narrow channel was reduced from 40 to 14 feet in depth, stranding 31 ships in an upstream port. The channel was dredged to allow passage of larger vessels, the first of a series of dredging operations conducted to keep Portland operating as a seaport. Pyroclastic flows (magma) with a volume of 6 square miles reached as far as 5 miles north of the crater, composed of multiple flows 3 to 30 feet thick. The cumulative depth of deposits reached 120 feet in places, traveling at speeds of up to 50 to 80 miles per hour at temperatures of at least 1,300 degrees fahrenheit.

The State Department of Game estimated nearly 7,000 big game animals (deer, elk, and bear) perished as well as all birds and most small mammals. Many burrowing rodents, frogs, salamanders, and crawfish managed to survive because they were below ground level or water surface when the disaster struck.

The Washington Department of Fisheries estimated 12 million Chinook and Coho salmon fingerlings were killed when hatcheries were destroyed. Another estimated 40,000 young salmon were lost when forced to swim through turbine blades of hydroelectric generators as reservoir levels along the Lewis River were kept low to accommodate possible mudflows and flooding.

Sadly, 57 human fatalities resulted directly from the combined effect of the blasts, including USGS employee David Johnston and modern-day folk hero Harry Truman. Truman's remains were recovered in his beloved Spirit Lake. An observatory and visitor information center was built and named in honor of Johnston on the ridge from where he kept volcano watch the morning of May 18, 1980, when the eruption occurred. The ridge also bears his surname.

12. MODERN PIONEERS MEET GUARDED GURU

True to the pioneer spirit of those who lived in this region before the advent of modern conveniences, the Gorge has continued to attract many adventurous souls who enjoy its resources as time marches on. Some have been more warmly welcomed than others by the existing community.

If it isn't obvious yet, perhaps this chapter will convince any doubters that, although the Columbia River Gorge has always been a small-town type of community, its history has been anything but dull. Its present is no different than its past, in this respect. What the modern-day Gorge lacks in population, it easily makes up for in opportunity. In fact, the obvious lack of overcrowding presents the best possibilities for enjoyment. And once in a while it creates an opportunity for unwanted trouble.

In 1981, enter Bhagwan Shree Rajneesh. Born Acharya Rajneesh in Kuchwada, India, he had already made some waves in his native country before he and his followers turned the tiny town of Antelope upside down. It would take two counties and the State of Oregon to put Antelope back on its feet.

Rajneesh was teaching philosophy at a university in India in the 1960s. A group of wealthy Bombay businessmen liked his message and began attending his meditation camps with their families in 1964. Rajneesh started additional camps as test-marketing facilities for his "enlightenment" campaign. The basic premise was that one could attain a state of enlightenment by meditating properly and regularly. The result of the enlightenment camps, aside from fattening Rajneesh's wallet, was a new phenomenon called dynamic meditation. In 1964, he founded the Neo-Sannyas International movement.

Changing his name to Bhagwan Shree Rajneesh in 1971, he added the use of several psychological methods to his meditation teachings, including rolfing, primal scream, and encounter-group therapies. Under his direction, a group of his sannyasins established a commune in an isolated location near Poona, teaching his followers to "become separate from" their day-to-day lives and surroundings. The movement was met with public disapproval by 1979 due to drug smuggling and prostitution acts committed by some of the Rajneesh disciples. After a young Hindu attempted to assault him in 1980, Rajneesh left the country without advance warning in May 1981, settling first in Montclair, New Jersey, with 18

A modern-day view of Arlington discloses its rural charm and direct connection to the Columbia River. Photo by Marlene Pointer.

disciples from India. He applied for permanent United States residency six months after his arrival, citing a need for medical treatment. By this time, his existing medical problems had improved greatly, raising questions with Immigration workers as to what medical treatment was actually required.

A nationwide search for commune property led Rajneesh and his disciples to the 65,000-acre Big Muddy ranch in rural Antelope, Oregon. In December 1982, Rajneesh was denied permanent resident status in the United States, as well as the desired classification of "religious leader." A year later he was granted a priority classification, but not a green card. The group began to erect new buildings almost immediately after arrival at Big Muddy, attempting to provide adequate housing for the masses expected to join the commune. They ran into opposition from the Antelope City Council, who refused to issue further building permits on the basis of the local water supply being inadequate to sustain operations that large. Things were about to turn ugly.

If the City of Antelope wouldn't cooperate, the Rajneeshees would just have to take control of the city. Despite Oregon's 30-day residency requirement for voting rights, the number of voting ranch-dwellers far exceeded the population of Antelope just months after their arrival. They managed to get elected to the Antelope City Council, the school board, and eventually even took over the school itself.

Between 1981 and 1983, the cult's numbers grew dramatically, giving the Rajneeshees even more local clout. Many members were young, intellectual types from wealthy families, including a surprising number of doctors, attorneys, and other professional people. An approximately equal number were still living the laid-back 1960s lifestyle The balance of the group were mostly curious college students either hoping for a great party or sincerely seeking a new truth in life. In those early years at the Big Muddy ranch, the property was incorporated as a town named Rajneeshpuram while attempts were made to disincorporate the City of Antelope. The attempt was successful with the April 1982 election. Next stop after that was to force the hand of Wasco County to allow the group free reign to do as they pleased. It would take a long list to please them, as it turned out.

The Rajneeshees, however, had overlooked a few things about the people of eastern Oregon, not the least of which was their pioneer background. Although the Rajneeshees were creating utter chaos in Antelope's city government, the cult's membership wasn't nearly big enough to overpower the county government—or the state. Although the county had authorized incorporation of Rajneeshpuram in November 1981, the local population and the state in general were getting a bad feeling about this group within a short time. In 1983 the state issued a temporary ruling that halted further expansion of the city of Rajneeshpuram until a determination could be made regarding the legal status of the city's incorporation. The city of Rajneeshpuram was largely on agricultural-use land, and state law seemed to indicate that a city could not incorporate on agricultural lands.

With all the lawyer-sannyasins that were living in the commune, the Rajneeshees had no hesitation about taking any and every issue to court. Hoping to break the system by perpetually filing lawsuits against any governing body or individual who got in the way of their progress, they spent a great deal of time in court. The entire group began wearing red garments and often created a blanket of red when they floated down the streets of The Dalles and Portland in their red robes. Part of their enlightenment program culminated with the enlightened one receiving a necklace made of exactly 108 beads, and a photo of the beloved Bhagwan prominently displayed as a pendant.

Rajneeshpuram had been substantially expanded by then, the organization having built a shopping mall, vegan restaurant, and even its own "contract station" post office. When the post office contract went out for public bid on September 29, 1982, a commune spokesman said the organization "receives and sends a pickup truck load of mail daily, with weekly postal expenses of $2,000 to $3,000."

With a population of about 600 year-round residents, the city had added a 4,500-foot paved airstrip, a 44-acre reservoir and an 88,000-square-foot meeting hall. Meanwhile, the Rajneeshees had purchased a hotel and a disco in downtown Portland. The hotel was named the Rajneesh Hotel and the disco was called Zorba the Buddha. According to former patrons, the disco was a great place to go for a good time, as long as service wasn't a priority. The businesses were staffed by the sannyasins who didn't already have professional occupations, and few of them had any work experience.

Some of the the expansion at Rajneeshpuram was deliberately done without the required building and land-use permits, often causing significant hardships for nearby residents. For example, farmlands and gardens in this arid part of the state need a regular irrigation source. If the usual source were to suddenly come up missing, it could create serious hardship, including crop or livestock loss and even bankruptcy. In building themselves a lovely private reservoir, the Rajneeshees requisitioned a body of water that had always hydrated the ranches downstream. Imagine the surprise of the neighboring ranchers, lifetime residents, when they discovered their canal had been blocked off for a reservoir without notice.

This was all just a little bit much, even for laid-back Oregonians, who were known for their live-and-let-live attitudes. Tensions were mounting across the state. The constant barrage of litigation and the flapping of red robes was all they could take. The international notoriety was fun for the locals at first, but even that ceased to be enjoyable after a few years.

The surrounding communities felt the commune had grown out of control. Rajneeshees believed the outlying community was bigoted and its religious intolerance out of control, so the cult arranged for its own elite "Peace Force" to patrol both inside and outside the ranch complex, and posted lookout stations. Entrances were all gated, with around-the-clock guards manning them, semi-automatic rifles in hand. When Rajneesh traveled in and around the ranch/city property by car he was escorted by armed guards and usually also by a militia-style helicopter. Anyone who dared rush the swami's vehicle had AK-47s or other serious weaponry aimed at them. But Rajneesh did want everyone to have a good time while they were at the ranch. The sannyasins and all guests were provided with AIDS avoidance kits, as encouragement to enjoy the commune's atmosphere of "free love," despite the recent outbreak of disease in the country.

The situation in Wasco County drew the attention of major media around the globe. Ted Koppel of "Nightline" interviewed the Rajneeshee spokesperson, "Ma Sheila," in 1983. Sheila was supposed to speak on behalf of Rajneesh, who had vowed complete silence recently for religious reasons. She was so angry that Koppel had to cut sound and even some of the video tape from most of the interview, because Sheila began yelling a string of obscenities, and somehow her middle finger was the only one that would stand up straight on her outstretched hand. She called community members unflattering names like racist, bigot, and redneck and said a good many things that won't be repeated in this book.

The first week of July 1984 brought some 5,800 potential disciples to the "First Annual World Celebration" at Rajneeshpuram, timed to honor the guru on "Guru Purnima Day," a traditional meeting time for disciples and their gurus. Travel arrangements were made through Rajneeshpuram, although it is unclear who ultimately paid for the dozens of chartered jets that landed in Portland or the hundreds of chartered bus trips between Portland International Airport and Rajneeshpuram. The number of converts to the Rajneesh commune was only a few hundred, which brought great disappointment to the swami.

Things came to a head in the fall of 1984, when the Rajneeshees sent out a group of recruiters to find and offer sanctuary to 3,000 to 4,000 homeless people around the nation in an attempt to fix the upcoming election results. These people were registered to vote as soon as they arrived at the commune, then kept occupied in a variety of ways until the elections were won. To keep non-Rajneeshees away from the polls, some of the members sprayed salmonella on

Two of the highest-ranking Rajneeshees in the late 1980s. On left, the guru himself, Baghwan Rajneesh. At right, his spokesperson "Ma Sheila." Multnomah County Jail mugshots.

salad bars in The Dalles restaurants, sending more than 700 people to the hospital with food poisoning. Secretary of State Norma Paulus set up a committee to review all voter registrations from the commune, the committee throwing out a large portion of the imported votes. A whole new crop of homeless people had been added to the Pacific Northwest population once the elections were over, although a small number of them did remain at Rajneeshpuram.

It isn't easy to summarize a memorable story like this. So many things happened between 1981 and 1985 that they have been covered in detail in more than one book devoted to the subject of the Rajneeshees. In the end, charges were brought against sannyasins for attempted murder of local United States attorney Charles Turner, the salmonella poisoning mentioned above, and a multi-bomb episode at the Rajneesh Hotel in Portland.

A 35-count federal indictment was handed down in October 1985, accusing Bhagwan Shree Rajneesh and several of his high-ranking disciples of arranging and performing bogus marriages for people from India who wanted to attain citizenship, and finally, his own immigration fraud. Attorney General Dave Frohnmeyer and several others had stood behind the distressed and poisoned residents of Wasco County throughout the entire ordeal, gathering information that would eventually be presented to federal authorities. Ma Sheila had already made a hasty departure for Switzerland by then, but she was located and spent two years in prison for her crimes. A total of 42 Rajneesh followers were charged, with 24 of them being convicted of various crimes.

At long last, the "Bagman," as he was known among the media members who covered this four-year saga, would be leaving eastern Oregon. He pleaded no contest to the immigration charges, agreed to immediate deportation, and paid a $400,000 fine. His health was substantially worse for the time he had spent in jail, so all parties considered it an adequate settlement. He changed his name again, this time to "Osho," upon return to his native country, and started a similar organization there. A short time before his sudden death in 1990, he named a group of 12 disciples to carry on his work through the Osho Foundation. The foundation is still in operation with its base in Poona, India.

One added point of interest is worth mentioning here regarding the infamous guru, in light of twenty-first century developments. According to one source, there is documented evidence of Rajneesh's involvement in a plot to fly an explosive-filled airliner into a large public building—the threat was reportedly made in the 1980s.

On a happier note, the Rajneeshpuram compound was abandoned until it was taken over in 1999 by YoungLife Ministries, a non-profit Christian organization. The property has been converted to a beautiful summer camp for high school teens. It currently accommodates more than 500 campers plus staff at any given time. Planned construction will add facilities enabling as many as 1,000 people to dine together, plus additional staff quarters. Current amenities for campers include numerous outdoor activities (mountain biking, ropes course, pond, snack bar, and portable sound system), a large outdoor pool with high and low dives, and a sports complex housing everything from pool tables to a climbing wall.

The Gorge's rich history has largely been preserved and protected, with many modern-day stewards hard at work to keep the valuable history accessible for the enjoyment of generations to come. This region has been further enhanced by the communities of individuals who now reside within it. Whether a visitor chooses to learn about Gorge history on foot, from the deck of a sternwheeler, at the wheel of a car, in an interpretive center or museum, or by reading a book like this one, there is an almost infinite number of places and time periods to tour. The region's natural resources made it a difficult part of the Oregon Trail, yet those same resources made it an ideal place to settle. Who, after all, could pass through such a dramatic, breathtaking landscape and not want to return? Those same qualities draw today's white-water rafters, windsurfers, runners, walkers, swimmers, rock hounds, boaters, campers, artists, and countless others to the Gorge time and time again.

It would be a gross understatement to say the Gorge has a lot to offer. The best description of this awe-inspiring area is a borrowed quote from novelist Thomas Wolfe: "It's a fabulous country—the one place where miracles not only happen, but where they happen all the time." Careful management of an amazing range of natural resources, plus historical preservation of cultural history, have made the Gorge a true treasure, in every sense of the word. The Gorge's caretakers have held her rich history dear, yet she forges on toward tomorrow in delighted anticipation of all that lies ahead. The frontier spirit is still palpable in the Columbia River Gorge.

NOTABLE GORGERS

Many of the Gorge's notable residents have been named elsewhere in this book, in sections containing anecdotes directly related to the time period in which they lived. There is an inevitable trade-off in a volume like this, where the author tries to find the right balance between going into full detail about an event and giving a simple summary of it. Literally thousands of people who were important to the history of the Gorge have not been named herein because their stories didn't fit into the timeline in a way that would make the book readable. But it seems appropriate to name some of the more famous people who were born in the Gorge, lived there, or made an especially notable visit.

Justin Chenoweth arrived in The Dalles in late 1848 with the First United States Mounted Rifles, although he was a civilian. He married Mary H. Vickers somewhere in Oregon Territory and they took a homestead west of The Dalles in 1852. Chenoweth, formerly known as Chenoweth Flat, and Chenoweth Creek are both named in Justin's honor. The creek flows across Chenoweth Flat, distributing its contents into the Columbia River near Crate's Point. It carried two other names prior to being called Chenoweth Creek: the Indians called it Thlemit and it was later called Olney Creek—named after Nathan Olney, the first private party to own a general store in the Gorge. The Chenoweth family left the local area in 1866 and Justin died in Portland March 16,1898.

Jeff Lahti, a 1975 graduate of Hood River Valley High School, was called up to play major league baseball in 1982 with the St. Louis Cardinals. This right-handed relief pitcher was drafted into the Cincinnati system in an earlier year but didn't see major league game time until he was traded to St. Louis.

Geneva Arlene McNicholl, also known as Mrs. Mac or Grandma Mac, was the state's oldest resident when she died January 22, 2002, at the age of 112 years, one month and 12 days. She lived independently, working in her garden and cooking her own meals until the age of 104, when she moved to a care center. Grandma Mac was born to Sylvester and Lovina (Henry) Grazer in Lafayette, Oregon, December 10, 1889. She married twice, to Harry Rogers and James McNicholl. After divorcing her second husband, in a very unusual move for the time, she continued to operate a grocery store/service station with her son on the Little White Salmon River until her retirement at age 76.

Mrs. McNicholl kept active in both body and mind until recently. She enjoyed hunting, fishing, travel, dancing, dinners with friends until recent years, and continued to participate in social and outdoor activities in her later years as opportunities arose. In the years immediately prior to her death, she was among but a small handful of people anywhere in the world who had personal memories of the days prior to the arrival of the airplane, automobile, and even the toaster.

Musician/band leader Doc Severinsen is probably best known for his long association with the Johnny Carson Show. He was born Carl H. Severinsen in 1927 and grew up in Arlington, dubbed "Little Doc" because his father was Doctor Carl Severinsen, a dentist. The elder Severinsen was an accomplished violinist and did not approve of his son's driving desire to play the trombone. In a town the size of Arlington (once known as Alkali), little Doc was hard pressed to find any musical instrument available, so he had to settle for a trumpet. A child prodigy, he was invited to play with the high school band after playing for only a week—at the age of seven. By the time he was 12 he had won the coveted Music Educators National Contest and was hired for a road tour with the Ted Fio Rito Orchestra while still in high school.

Doc completed his education and then toured with the biggest of the big bands: Tommy Dorsey, Benny Goodman, and Charlie Barnet, then settled in as an NBC staff musician in New York in 1949. He joined the Tonight Show orchestra in 1962, becoming the band's director in 1967. He still conducts the Phoenix Symphony, the Buffalo Philharmonic, and several other orchestras throughout the nation. He has recorded more than 30 big band, jazz fusion, and classical albums and plays regularly with the former Tonight Show band, which is now known as Doc Severinsen and his Big Band.

Harold Lenoir Davis, Pulitzer Prize–winning author, was born north of Roseburg at Rone's Mill in the foothills of the Cascades. His family moved to Antelope and then to The Dalles where his father worked as an itinerant teacher. The elder Mr. Davis then became principal, enabling the family to remain in The Dalles for the next 20 years. As is often the case for writers, Harold worked many other jobs before gaining recognition as a writer. His first writing successes were in the form of poetry, gaining encouragement later on by H.L. Mencken to pursue prose. He wrote the prize-winning book *Honey in the Horn* in 1935 while in Mexico on a Gugenheim Fellowship. It is an epic novel about homesteading in Oregon around the turn of the century. Beulah Land (1949) and The Distant Music (1957) were some of his later works. His trademark style was an honest portrayal of men and women on the frontier, which differed greatly from the more common cowboy heroes portrayed by other writers of the day.

Pearl Zane Gray, who changed the spelling of his surname to Grey when he began to write books, visited the Gorge several times during the first two decades of the twentieth century. He stopped to stay with his younger cousin Joseph Aden Gray near the foot of the Cascades. When Joe Gray was in story-telling mode at family reunions, he talked about his youthful years on Juniper Flat in southern Wasco County, and often would take the listener on up through the early years of his marriage to Amy Hix. His stories of those years always included mention of his cousin Zane Grey, the noted author of western novels. He said Zane looked him up because they were cousins, and Joe would often relate a story to Zane that would become fodder for a chapter in one of the next books. The remote regions in the western states were substantially behind as compared to what was happening in the Midwest, so Joe's early memories and those told to him by his father were very valuable to the writer.

Unfortunately, by the time anyone in the family thought to ask Joe exactly how he and Zane were related through Joe's father, he couldn't recall that Zane ever told him anything specific. Joe's father died when Joe was just a lad, and his place in Zane Grey's family remains unknown to this day. How the cousins became acquainted for the first time is also unknown to any living descendants of either man. As a token of his respect for his cousin, Joe named one of his sons Zane Gray.

Linus Pauling, chemist, author, and two-time Nobel Prize winner (1954, 1962) spent about half his childhood in Condon. He attended grade school there when his father had a drug store in town, the family making a move to Portland in time for Pauling to graduate from Washington High School there. He obtained his bachelor's degree from Oregon State College in 1922. Pauling was a physical chemist, toiling with the minutia of atoms and molecules. Some of his research led to advances in understanding sickle cell anemia and vitamin C, and he helped develop a molecular explanation for the process of anesthesia.

Thomas Condon, geologist and paleontologist, was the first scientific investigator of the fossil beds of the John Day area. He traveled around Cape Horn from New York to land at Portland in 1852 and was ordained as a Congregational church minister. He served congregations in several locations west of the Gorge and moved to The Dalles in 1862. He served as pastor of The Dalles church from 1862 to 1870. He became the state's first geologist while teaching at Pacific University in 1872, then was appointed as the first geology professor at the University of Oregon when it was established in 1876. He remained there until 1907.

Condon's book *The Two Islands* formed the foundation for the study of Oregon's historical geology. Often referred to as the "Grand Old Man of Science" in the state of Oregon, he left his fossil collections to the two schools named above. The main visitor's center at the John Day Fossil Beds National Monument, as well as Condon Hall at the University of Oregon, are named in his honor. The town of Condon in Gilliam County is named for his nephew, attorney Harvey C. Condon, who lived in Alkali (now Arlington).

BIBLIOGRAPHY

An Illustrated History of Central Oregon. Spokane: Western Historical Publishing Company, 1905.

An Illustrated History of Klickitat, Yakima, & Kittitas Counties (Washington). Chicago: Interstate Publishing Company, 1904 (*Part IV, History of Klickitat County*)

Beckham, Stephen Dow. *The Indians of Western Oregon: This Land Was Theirs*. Arago Books, 1977.

————. *Requiem for a People: The Rogue Indians and the Frontiersmen*. University of Oklahoma Press, 1971. Second printing by Oregon State University, 1997.

Beeson, John. A *Plea for the Indians*. Ye Galleon Press, 1982.

Beeson to True Californian, 12 August 1856, in United States, Office of Indian Affairs, Letters Received by the Office of Indian Affairs, 1824–1880, National Archives Microcopy 234, Roll 609, NADP Document D40.

Beeson to Editor, *New York Tribune*, 30 September 1856, in United States, Office of Indian Affairs, Letters Received by the Office of Indian Affairs, 1824–1880, National Archives Microcopy 234, Roll 609, NADP Document D43.

Bensell, Royal A. *All Quiet on the Yamhill: The Civil War in Oregon*. Gunther Barth, ed. University of Oregon Books, 1959.

Brantley and Myers. *Mount St. Helens—From the 1980 Eruption to 1996*: USGS Fact Sheet 070–97.

Burkhardt, D.C. Jesse. *Backwoods Railroads: Branchlines and Shortlines of Western Oregon*. Pullman, Washington: Washington State University Press, 1994.

Carey, Charles Henry. *History of Oregon*. Pioneer Historical Publishing Company,1922.

Caswell, John Edwards. "The Prohibition Movement in Oregon to the Adoption of Statewide Prohibition in 1914." M.A. thesis, University of Oregon, 1937.

Clark, Malcolm. *The War on the Webfoot Saloon & Other Tales of Feminine Adventures*. Portland, Oregon: Oregon Historical Society Press, 1969.

Culp, Edwin D. *Early Oregon Days*. Caldwell, Idaho: The Caxton Printers, Limited, 1987

Davenport, T.W. "Recollections of an Indian Agent." *Oregon Historical Quarterly*, March, June, September, and December, 1907

Due, John F., and French, Giles. *Rails to the Mid-Columbia Wheatlands: The*

Columbia Southern and Great Southern Railroads and the Development of Sherman and Wasco Counties, Oregon. University Press of America, 1979.

Due, John F., and Rush, Frances Juris. *Roads and Rails South From the Columbia*. Bend, Oregon: Maverick Publications, Inc., 1991.

Gaston, Joseph. *The Centennial History of Oregon—1811–1912*. Volume I. Chicago: S.J. Clarke Publishing Company, 1912.

Harris, Bruce. *The History of Wasco County*. Unpublished, located in Wasco County Library. 1983.

Hendrickson, James E. *Joe Lane of Oregon: Machine Politics and the Sectional Crisis, 1845–1861*. Yale University Press, 1967.

History of the Columbia River Valley From The Dalles to the Sea. Volumes I and II. Chicago: S.J. Clarke Publishing Company, 1912.

History of the Pacific Northwest: Oregon and Washington. Volume II. Portland: North Pacific History Company, 1889.

Hoxie, Frederick E. *A Final Promise: The Campaign to Assimilate the Indians, 1880–1920*. Lincoln: University of Nebraska Press, 1984.

Kirkwood, Charlotte Matheny. *Into the Eye of the Setting Sun*. Available on Windows-compatible floppy disk from Walt Davies, 14125 Fishback Rd., Monmouth, OR 97361

Jackman, E.R., and Long, R.A. *The Oregon Desert*. Caldwell, Idaho: The Caxton Printers, Limited, 1973.

J. Ross Browne to Commissioner of Indian Affairs, 4 December 1857, in United States, Office of Indian Affairs, Letters Received by the Office of Indian Affairs, 1824–1880, National Archives Microcopy 234, Roll 611, NADP Document D61.

Lyman, Horace S. *History of Oregon*. North Pacific Publishing Society, 1903.

Maupin Times, early issues.

McNeal, William H. *History of Wasco County, Oregon*. The Dalles: Wasco County Pioneers Association, 1950.

Milne, Hugh. *Bhagwan: The God That Failed*. Saint Martin's Press.

Nash, Wallis. *Oregon: There and Back in 1877*. Oregon State University Press, 1976.
————. *Two Years in Oregon*. D. Appleton and Company, 1882.

Nesmith, James W. "A Reminiscence of the Indian War, 1853." *Oregon Historical Quarterly*, 1906.

Newsom, David. *David Newsom: The Western Observer 1805–1882*. Oregon Historical Society, 1972.

Nielsen, Lawrence E., Doug Newman, and George McCart. *Pioneer Roads in Central Oregon*. Bend, Oregon: Maverick Publications, 1985.

New York Times, March 11, 1998 page A21.

Nelson, Ray. *Memoirs of an Oregon Moonshiner*. Caldwell, Idaho: Caxton Printers, 1976.

O'Donnell, Terence. *An Arrow in the Earth: General Joel Palmer and the Indians of Oregon*. Oregon Historical Society, 1991.

Potter, Miles F. *Oregon's Golden Years*. Caldwell, Idaho: The Caxton Printers,

Limited, 1976.

Price, Richard L. *Newport, Oregon: 1866–1936, Portrait of a Coastal Resort*. Lincoln County Historical Society, 1975.

Prucha, Francis Paul. *The Great Father: The United States Government and the American Indians*. University of Nebraska Press, 1984.

Rees, Helen Guyton. *Shaniko, From Wool Capital to Ghost Town*. Portland: Binsford and Mort, 1982.

Robbins, Harvey. "Journal of the Rogue River War." *Oregon Historical Quarterly* Volume 34 (December 1933), pp.345–358.

Scott, Harvey W. *History of the Oregon Country*, Volume I. Cambridge: The Riverside Press, 1924.

Shaniko Leader, Illustrated Annual. Volume II, Number 38. Shaniko, Oregon. January, 1902. Available at the Oregon Historical Society.

Tilling, Topinka, and Swanson. *Eruptions of Mount St. Helens: Past, Present, and Future*. USGS Special Interest Publication, 1990.

Trennert, Robert A, Jr. *Alternative to Extinction: Federal Indian Policy and the Beginnings of the Reservation System, 1846–1851*. Philadelphia: Temple University Press, 1975.

Victor, Frances Fuller. *The Early Indian Wars of Oregon*. Salem: Frank C. Baker, State Printer, 1894.

This traveler is about to be delighted with the magnificent treasure waiting just up the road at Vista House. The view is spectacular and the location is a beautiful example of ageless architecture. Courtesy of Hood River County Historical Museum.

INDEX

1891 Fire, 83–85, 87, 91

1894 Flood, 88–91, 93

Antelope, 61–63, 71, 100, 102, 104, 114, 147–149, 154

Arlington, 22, 74, 104, 148, 154, 155

Balch, Rev. F.H., 75

Barlow Road, 27, 42, 43, 45, 59, 60, 110

Bigelow, W.D., 58

Biggs, 72, 79, 91, 102, 104

Bingen, 48, 59, 74, 75, 89, 91, 112, 113

Booth, John P., 61

Bridge of the Gods, 13, 14, 75, 88, 134

Brookhouse, John, 65

Brooks, Samuel, 61

Butcher, W.R., 61

Butler, Dan, 57

Cascade Locks, 12, 61, 78, 91, 94, 110, 111, 118, 134, 135

Cayuse, 15, 29, 30, 32, 33, 97

Celilo, 14–16, 18, 110, 129, 133, 15, 25, 31

Chief Kamaiakin, 47, 48

Chief Paulina, 63

Coe, Nathaniel, 48

Columbia Southern Railroad, 73, 113

Comfort, E.B., 61

Condon, James B., 61

Cook, Mary Frances Scott, 37

Cowne, E.G., 57, 58

Craig, P., 57, 58

Cross Hollows, 62, 72, 73

Curtis, A.H., 58

Daugherty, Dave, 64

Dee, 111

DeMoss, W.L., 58

Deschutes River, 30, 43, 60, 62, 63, 78, 86, 104, 105

Donnell, Camilla, 61

Donnell, Zelek, 60, 61

Dufur, 67, 104, 106

Duniway, Abigail Scott, 36, 38

Eaton, Nate 80

Floyd, Ed, 65

Ford, Ninevah, 21–25

French, Joshua, 61, 83

Fulton, Frank, 64, 65

Gates, Colonel N.H., 57, 58, 109

Gibson, Ed, 65

Gilliam, Cornelius, 26, 30–33

Gilliam County, 57, 78, 117, 155

Goldendale, 70, 128

Gordon, Tom, 64

Grass Valley, 60, 79, 117

Hall, R., 57

Haller, Major Granville O., 47

Helm, C.I. (Charlie), 65

Hinton, James E., 72, 73

Hinton, Richard, 72

Hood River, 46, 48, 49, 57, 70, 75, 78, 79, 86, 89, 91, 110–112, 114–116, 118, 122, 126, 127, 133, 142

Hudson's Bay, 18, 20, 23, 30, 35

Humason, Captain Orlando, 49, 57, 61

Hunsaker, Jacob, 75

Huntington, B.S., 61

Hurst, Malinda Davis, 39, 49, 65
Imperial Stock Ranch, 72
Isaacs, H.T., 58
Jenkins, William, 48
Joslyn, Erastus 48, 59
Joslyn, Thomas, 60, 61
Keeney, Jonathan, 50–51, 58
Kelly, Colonel James K., 58
Kirkwood, Charlotte Matheny, 24, 27, 33, 76
Klickitat, 13, 14, 16, 48, 59, 93, 128, 129
Laurel Hill, 39, 44, 59
Lee, Major H.A. J., 30
Liebe, Geo., 67–68
Lockley, Fred, 37
Lyle, 40, 75
Maryhill, 91, 121, 128, 129
Maupin, 62, 63, 100, 102, 104
McAuliffe, James, 58
McCormick, B.F., 57, 58
McDonald, Fred, 61
McFarland, E.B., 61
McLoughlin, Dr. John, 38, 40
Meigs, C.R., 57
Memaloose Island, 133
Mill Creek, 68, 90
Moody, Governor Zenas, 61, 104
Moody, W.C., 58
Mosier, 86, 89, 93, 124, 125
Mount St. Helens, 11, 14, 142–146
Mount Hood, 11, 12, 14, 18–20, 66–68, 111, 116, 143
Multnomah Falls, 70, 117, 122
Nesmith, J.W., 21, 49
Nixon, A.J., 58, 92
Olney, Nathan, 49, 153
Oregon Steam Navigation Co., 61, 114
Oregon Trail, 21–26, 40–45, 86, 104, 152
Palmer, Joel, 49, 53
Pearson, Bill, 65
Pearson, Jim, 65
Penfield, E.S., 61
Pentland, Robert, 61
Portland, 13, 41, 48, 78, 82, 90, 109, 114, 115, 117, 118, 121, 122, 124, 126–130,
138, 141, 142, 146, 149–151, 153, 155
Price, Albert Jay, 64, 65, 78, 79
Rajneesh, Bhagwan Shree, 147–152
Reeder, George, 64
Robinson, Mrs. E.R., 61
Rogue River, 46, 49, 50, 51, 53, 54
Roscoe, R.A., 61
Rufus, 91, 117
Savage, Albert L., 78
Shaniko, 62, 72, 73, 101, 102, 104, 113, 114
Sherman County, 57, 60, 78, 117, 118, 137
Silky Smith, 67
Stilwell, W.D., 61
Sylvester, O., 61, 84
Tenny, W.A., 60
The Dalles, 21, 22, 29, 30, 32, 33, 35, 36, 39, 48, 49, 51, 57, 58, 60, 62–64, 67, 68, 70–72, 77, 78, 81, 83, 84, 86–91, 93, 95, 96, 98–102, 104–108, 110, 112–114, 116, 121, 124, 125, 129, 130, 132, 135–138, 149, 151, 153–155
Thompson, R.R., 58
Umatilla House, 58, 89–93, 100, 102
Waiilatpu, 29, 32, 33
Waldron, H.J., 61
Walker, Bill, 64
Walker, Joe, 64
Warner's Landing, 59, 75
Wasco County, 20, 46, 49, 56, 57, 61, 78, 80, 112, 114, 115, 135, 137, 149, 150, 151, 154
Waters, James, 30, 31, 33
White River Falls, 2
White Salmon, 48, 49, 59, 60, 70, 74, 75, 85–87, 111–113, 117, 126, 141, 142
Whitman family, 20, 29, 30, 32, 33, 46
Willamette Valley, 9, 20, 22, 24, 27, 29, 36, 53, 57, 66, 71–73, 113, 114, 117
Wright, George W., 49, 50
Yakima, 32, 46–49, 51, 54, 79, 128